# TIME OR TOO LATE

## CHASING THE DREAM
## OF A PROGRESSIVE CHRISTIAN FAITH

GRETTA VOSPER

Decorative Fonts: Orna 1
Listemageren 1997 - bibliste@post2.tele.dk
Headings: Articulat CF: utilitarian sans serif
Connary Fagen Type Design - http://connary.com/
Text: Garamond

Published by File 14: PostPurgical Resources, Toronto, ON

Time or Too Late
Chasing the Dream of a Progressive Christian Faith.
Paperback: ISBN 978-0-9737752-5-9
Electronic Book: ISBN 978-0-9737752-6-6

# TABLE OF CONTENTS

## PREFACE

The beginning of a new endeavor is always a heady time. If it is something personal like a program of study, a move, or a new relationship, you have a lot of control over what transpires. Not total control, of course, but a significant portion is under your own command.

When that endeavor is the beginning of an organization intended to hold back the receding sea of faith, however, control is the last thing you can expect. You are able, at best, to take only the measure of what you know and see and understand. The rest unfurls as it will and the best you can do is hang on, try to discern and make sense of events and their implications as they come, and trim the sails as you journey.

So it was when we braved the launch of the Canadian Centre for Progressive Christianity, encouraged by the founder of The Center for Progressive Christianity (TCPC), the late Reverend Jim Adams, and a handful of explorers cast adrift by their traditional faith communities. Jim, Bishop John Shelby Spong, and I addressed a packed auditorium early in November, 2004, and we were off on an adventure. We launched an organization and I forged relationships with two men that provided me guidance, insight, and courage for what was to come.

This book contains some of the work that came about as the result of that night, the events that followed, and the intense journey that was the Canadian Centre for Progressive Christianity. I was privileged to cross the country sharing a vision of a church beyond belief with congregations, communities, and leaders and to speak at each of our conferences. Here you will find a record of some of the things I said, noting, I am sure, the shift in perspective that the years brought. Both of my books, *With or Without God: Why the Way We Live is More Important than What We Believe* and *Amen: What Prayer Can Mean in a World beyond Belief* were written out of the experience of working with the community at West Hill, the many Canadians who shared their frustrations and dreams with me, and the work of this Centre we had created.

Even before it was born, however, controversy was abundant. At the second meeting of those interested in creating a network, we struggled over the name of the new organization. The group debated the use of the word "Christianity" with almost half wanting to leave the term behind. And we looked for alternatives to "progressive" but found every other possibility equaled troubling, try as we might to find a term that didn't suggest others were closed-minded, regressive, or laggards. In the end, the Canadian Centre for Progressive Christianity was chosen by a tiny margin, imposing two highly controversial words on an organization whose work would be equally so.

Within a year of our launch, the Board was working on its own Eight Points. Jim Adams had encouraged the many networks his work had instigated – the United Kingdom, Ireland, New Zealand, and Australia – to develop their own statements. He had been adamant that the TCPC's Eight Points of Progressive Christianity not become a new creed and entrench themselves in the minds of progressives around the globe. Better, he argued, to have a variety of statements to represent regional and national differences.

Our Eight Points diverged significantly from those of the TCPC, much to the chagrin of Canadians who had already embraced TCPC's points. We were accused of "stealing" progressive Christianity from Canadians and imposing our own interpretations upon the country. While we refuse the claim that we imposed anything upon anyone, we certainly had created points that stood apart from those of our American progressive brothers and sisters.

TCPC, after the leadership of Jim Adams, had existed up until that time primarily to invite people *into* the church. The purpose of the resources developed and the points articulated was to create an open atmosphere within churches that would allow new participants to feel welcome enough to explore more modern understandings of Christianity that reinterpreted ecclesial doctrinal statements. Of course, those statements were softened considerably by the kind of contemporary critical scholarship produced by the Jesus Seminar and taught in congregations connected with TCPC. The ultimate success of TCPC's work was made evident when previously skeptical newcomers became members, assuming and accepting those same doctrinal statements in order to do so.

That had never been the impetus for the Canadian version of TCPC. Having grown out of a decidedly more liberal Christian environment than the US, the CCPC sought to encourage congregations to relinquish the use of traditional Christian language while maintaining the values and principles progressive communities of faith often embraced. It was very much the product of the community out of which the organization had grown, West Hill United Church. There, for several years, the community had been developing what it now refers to as a theologically barrier-free space. Rather than creating a more open environment that would invite newcomers to embrace indoctrination, CCPC set a path that protected newcomers from it, allowing participation without assent to doctrinal statements. Those who had moved beyond traditional religious beliefs or who had never held them at all, would not be required to learn religious language in order to participate. As one CCPC clergy member once noted, her service needed to be clean enough that someone without any Christian understanding at all would "get it" just the way it was.

We did not choose an easy path. While the CCPC drew significant crowds to our conferences and many would gather to hear of our work as we travelled across Canada, very few congregations actually undertook to really lean in to the work of removing ecclesial language from their Sunday services. Our first conference, in Oshawa, prompted a colleague to twist the conference title into a sign preaching reliance on Jesus; his church was just down the street from the conference location. Although many clergy became comfortable acknowledging their doubts or unbelief to congregants during the week, Sunday remained locked in traditions that barred the doors to those for whom they no longer had meaning. Those congregations that did make change, often suffered as a result. And rather than bring people into the church, the CCPC may have found more success in unwittingly giving them permission to leave, something we had never intended to do.

In the opening piece, you'll find the theme for our launch, "It's time." Perhaps it was. Twelve years later, I am able to look back and wonder if the work of transforming church, transitioning it beyond the doctrinal beliefs it held but no longer taught as literal in its theological colleges was already too late. Indeed, I've suggested to colleagues and supporters that the work was two or three generations behind schedule in Canada. I have little optimism for the success of any Canadian congregation that might choose to begin the work we believed was crucial to the development of a progressive Christian faith at this late date in the life of the liberal church. American congregations are a completely different story since they do not lack the generations of involvement that Canadian churches do.

I do not believe, however, that it is too late for the liberal church anywhere to recognize the power of the legacy it might yet leave to generations that have no interest in church. There are, of course, many Gen Xers and Millennials who are terrifically engaged in meaningful justice work but too many others are indifferent to what goes on around them, living in isolation or small urban tribes, their well-being compromised, and their engagement significantly diminished from what their parents' may have been. Liberal churches have much to offer. Indeed, a wholesale transfer of intellectual, social, leadership, and even financial capital to secular communities could take place.

But that is another dream for another book. I leave you to this one. May it remind you of the incredible work we have done and the commitment we must each make the future that yet lies before us.

> What you want.
> No, what I want.
> Maybe you'll want what it is I want
> or I'll want what it is you want
> or you'll just want for me what I want
> or I'll just want for you what you want.
> We can't stop wanting what we want
> but maybe we can trim it down a bit,
> share …
> or something like that. [1]

---

[1] Gretta Vosper, *We All Breathe* (Toronto: File 14, 2012)

# It's Time

*CCPC Launch, November, 2004*

We come to this moment in time, called by a very long list of voices, and it has been many, many years, decades, even centuries, that those voices have been calling us. We have been urged here by those who have been examining scripture for years and finding that its origins, together with the contradictions and repetitions within it, must explain it as the construction of human hands.

We have been called here by those who noted that the defense of a document's truth cannot be found exclusively within itself.

We have been called by those who have sifted through the sands of the Middle East, eager to find some kind of proof for the burden of both testaments, and finding, once those sands have filtered through their fingers, few grains of fact remaining.

We have been called by those whose questions about the nature of reality we could not answer or, if we did, our answers held no meaning for them.

We have been called by those who have found too many of the Bible's moral messages, in the light of the call to love one's neighbor, worse than irrelevant, but actually life denying.

We have been called by those who were excommunicated from the established church for thinking outside the church's interpretation of faith, for daring to confront, to argue, to think daringly, and to act bravely.

We have been called by those who, outside of our version of Christian legitimacy, have still lived out the values of love and justice, compassion and forgiveness.

We have been called time and again to meet their challenges, and even when we have listened, too often we have shied away.

Listen to this particular call:

> *I suspect that we stand on the brink of a period in which it is going to become increasingly difficult to know what the true defense of Christian truth requires. ... I believe we are being called, over the years ahead, to far more than a restating of traditional orthodoxy in modern terms. Indeed, if our defense of the Faith is limited to this, we shall find in all likelihood that we have lost out to all but a tiny religious remnant. A much more radical recasting, I would judge, is demanded, in the process of which the most fundamental categories of our theology—of God, of the supernatural, and of religion itself – must go into the melting. Indeed, though we shall not of course be able to do it, I can at least understand what those mean who urge that we should do well to give up using the word "God" for a generation, so impregnated has it become with a way of thinking we may have to discard it if the Gospel is to signify anything.*

These words were penned in 1963 as the preface for the small but enormously provocative book, *Honest to God*, by John A. T. Robinson. Robinson was the Bishop of Woolwich in South London when he wrote his book, provoked by the ideas of Paul Tillich. Robinson's words came as freshness upon a bleak and sterile ecclesial back-drop to the many who wished to see his challenge accepted by the church—those passionate about what the church might be and what it could do in a world filled with conflict and strife. He was vilified for his vision and his challenge to organized Christianity. Yet he ended the preface of his groundbreaking book with this line:

> *The one thing of which I am fairly sure is that, in retrospect, [my words] will be seen to have erred in not being nearly radical enough.*

And, those heartened by Robinson, too, have called to us and continue to do so.

Robert Funk founded the Westar Institute in 1986, as an advocate for religious literacy. It flung wide the doors of academia so that the public could access the quest for the historical Jesus, trying to discover who the man said to have started all this really was and what he might have really been intending to do. That quest has been engaged in by scholars such as John Dominic Crossan, Marcus Borg, and Karen Armstrong.

Others have sought to understand our faith from a different perspective. They have called to us to consider that the concept of *Kristos*, a rich and deep expression of the longing for a just and peace-filled world, existed long before it was embedded in the stories of the life of a man remembered as Jesus of Nazareth. The works of Godfrey Higgins, Gerald Massey, and Alvin Boyd Kuhn, recently remembered to us by Tom Harpur, and those of Susan Adams and John Salmon, these works, these voices, too, call us to this place today.

Brian Swimme and Matthew Fox, for over twenty years, have been calling us to cast aside ecclesial depictions of life as a debased and transitory journey toward everlasting pleasures or tortures, and to see creation, including our human bodies, as a thing of wonder and beauty. Carter Heyward opens our eyes to equity issues and calls our hearts to recognize that it is God lurching in our stomachs when injustice causes us despair and rage.

Richard Holloway, former Bishop of Edinburgh, argues that human thinking influences our understanding of God, and therefore even the original writers of Scripture. His book, *Doubts and Loves*, proposes that the ordination of women picked at the fabric of biblical inerrancy and was perhaps what pulled out that first stitch, thus beginning the unravelling of what seemed a previously perfect, seamless garment.

In 2002, Andrew Furlong, a priest in Ireland, came before an ancient tradition in the form of a heresy trial for making this same call to us. His resignation, personal preservation from a frightened church, is also a call to us.

Don Cupitt has bravely and profoundly called to us from many points in his developing understanding of religion, challenging us to make dramatic but deeply liberating and healing changes in our concepts, our wording, our practices. Lloyd Geering, even into his late 80s continues to provoke us with his insights into the development of Christianity and the world in which we live, calling for honest, open scholarship. Calls to integrity come from James Barr, David Boulton, Burton Mack, and many others.

Jim Adams, throughout his ministry at St. Mark's Episcopal Church on Capitol Hill in Washington, brought practical reality to the words being penned by scholars, building the faith community on progressive principles of Christianity. And Bishop John Shelby Spong, first recipient of the Westar Institute's "John A. T. Robinson Award" for his unrelenting honesty in both spoken and written word, in the face of massively difficult ecclesial and social issues presented to the church, continues his call to us this evening.

Over forty years of scholarship and argument later, we cannot shrink from Robinson's vision. We, too, must look at it directly and rise to his challenge, recasting our understanding of Christianity, examining the structures that have supported it, clearing away those things that would keep us from seeing it clearly; for it's time to step more and more boldly into the realities of this world as we experience them, to open ourselves to an honest critique of our Christian heritage, and to expose ourselves to the light of new understandings that so many have placed before us. It's time.

9

## A spiritual dimension

We see all human beings as having a spiritual dimension to their lives. And it is within that dimension of our lives that we interact with that which we would call the spirit, the ground of all being, the divine. When we have constructed dogma about the divine and created rituals with which to relate to it, we have called it "religion." Religion seems to be mandated by our peculiar human need to make sense of our world. And so we construct our institutions and traditions, for our time, and according to beliefs as we understand them.

But it does not and cannot stand that one generation's idea of the appropriate approach to their particular concept of the divine must hold for the next generation. Just as every other field of knowledge and wisdom has changed as we have learned, our faith communities have not only the freedom, but the supremely important responsibility to work at our message and our expression of it - to align and realign it with the best, the highest, the healthiest vision we can develop of the sacredness of life, the sacredness of community. We, too, must take up that task and work to create a world in which each person's right to find their own way is honored, whether it involves ancient or contemporary rituals or traditions, religious or secular means, and we challenge ourselves to be open to new understandings of the divine as they are made known to us.

The Canadian Centre for Progressive Christianity has been created to help us, you and me, meet the challenges that our world presents us.

## Language and the nature of faith

For generations, working within the confines of traditional Christianity – whether as lay leaders or as ordered ministry personnel – has meant operating in a language of faith that grew out of a beautifully rich belief system, a religion known and celebrated through millennia. The exquisite nature of that language of faith, be it music, prayer, imagery, ritual, art, has brought untold comfort and security to a vast host of believers. For that reason, it has become very powerful.

However, there exists another vast host of people who searched for meaning in the midst of a chaotic world, who struggled, but failed to embrace the things Christian authorities called "truth," for whom healing and a truth they can embrace may yet be distant from them. For these people, the view of history held by the church, the language that was intended to bring stability, beauty, and understanding, has been for them a strong and inviolable barrier to Christianity and its communities of faith. Even though we on the inside may have derived a certain amount of comfort in glossing over discrepancies, sticking with familiar, if no-longer-believed statements of faith, and trying to explain the peculiar words and requirements to newcomers, I believe it is no longer helpful or healthful for us to continue to do so. If we are to be an influence for good, for comfort, for strength, or for growth, we must use the language of those who come to us, not require that they come to understand ours. *It's time.*

I am not talking about calling the sanctuary "the Celebration Room" or the narthex "the lobby" (although that may help some people more easily find where to hang their coats). I'm not talking just about inclusive language. I'm referring to letting go of words and statements and concepts that reiterate dogma we do not any longer (or maybe never did) truly believe ourselves, let alone require that others do so.

I'm referring to a conscientious clearing of the house of faith of language that suggests salvation from hell in return for a belief in the sacrifice of Jesus for our sins. I'm talking about being willing to give up singing hymns – no matter how dear to our hearts – that reiterate that sacrificial bargain, and celebrate Christianity's march across the world, bringing light to all the nations. I'm urging us to carefully, reverently stop referring to God as someone who directs or does not direct us, grants or does not grant our requests, saves or does not save a loved one from harm for reasons that God may choose but that we, most certainly will not understand, yet must accept as evidence of God's wisdom, power, and love.

11

I'm suggesting that we boldly, comfortably, write our own sacred wisdom, gleaning from Scripture all that is life-enhancing, but none that is not – and stretching ourselves to discover new expressions of the Spirit, new challenges to our community. We need to be ruthlessly honest, to state who we are, what we believe or don't, what we don't yet understand, and work together to discover new ways to find meaning in the world, new strength to engage its too inhumane systems, new joy in the experience that we call life.

We have much on which to build. We hold deeply sacred beliefs about the value of life. We hold deeply sacred beliefs about the value of community. We hold deeply sacred beliefs about our responsibility for each other. None of these will be left behind. And, if for some of us, this talk is still about stepping into the unknown, then I believe that we will find, as Overton says, that there will be ground beneath our feet or we will have wings to fly. *It's time.*

## The plan

Over the course of the next few months and years, we hope to be able to provide, through our website, and perhaps publications, accessible tools for use in study, worship, and community leadership. We hope to inspire congregational leaders to let go of their traditional liturgy, or traditional liturgy restated in postmodern language, and to reach within themselves to the core of their being from which can well up incredibly rich and fresh language, imagery, poetry, music. It will not be easy – many of us have become numb to some of our own creative instincts – but it is essential.

There are so many points in our lives that touch the spiritual realm. We look to the spiritual to gain strength, to evaluate our lives and refocus on those things we want to place at the centre of them as important, to recognize and give thanks for those who have touched us and brought clarity or peace to our souls, to reconnect with that which is precious to us – to name it sacred, holy. I speak of birth, coming of age, declarations of love and commitment, the changes inherent in the passing of years, the end of life as we know it. We hope to be able to provide resources that will add to those points in ways that dignify our common search and celebrate life's holy moments.

And we hope to offer study resources and ideas for those of you who may yet and for some time search for but not find communities of faith that speak a language that is open to your thought, your spiritual quest, your experience of the Divine. Those resources will encourage critical thinking, the gathering together of groups and the formation of communities that can engage in conversation about the big things, issues that matter – values, meaning, relationships – the things we call "of the Spirit."

In many communities of faith, the guiding light has been some form of church authority, based on literal or metaphorical Scripture, accepted traditional formulas, or official pronouncements. May we now look to the only light that can guide us into the freedom of faith and the privilege of responsibility – the truth revealed to us in the light of love. May we see and know that spirit within us, may it shine forth in us, and from us.

By the light of the sun and the glow of the moon
we can see the nat'ral world all around us.
But the world of the spirit is a world of mystery
and nat'ral light won't help us to see.

In the light of love our lives have meaning.
In the light of love our purpose shines.
Whenever there is justice to be dared,
compassion to be shared, this is our calling
in the light of love.

*Refrain:*
So lift it up, hold it high, write it clear across the sky.
Burn it deep within your soul,
live it well and live it whole
for nothing more is needed but nothing less will do,

for nothing else can take the place of love.

In the light of love our lives have dignity.
In the light of love our purpose shines.
To celebrate the beauty ev'rywhere
with deep respect and care, this is our calling
in the light of love.
*Refrain*

Not our forms, not our creeds
neither plans nor empty deeds,
no nothing else can take the place of love.
Not our status, not our health, not inheritance or wealth;
no, nothing else can take the place of love.
*Refrain*
© 2004 R. Scott Kearns

There is purpose to our work. Our world calls us to it. The earth, so filled with beauty, with gifts of peace and delight, is also filled with misery, with violence, with a futile busyness that steals our time to feel and to care. Were we to look, we would find in every corner, even in our own homes, places where love is needed in much, much greater quantities than it is ever found.

If we are convinced of the profound significance of each person as an infinitely precious being, and I believe that we can only be convinced of such a thing, we must then dream and plan and work toward positive change to enhance the well-being of self, others, and the whole of creation – to be intentional about building love into all those corners of despair.

To encourage the ongoing search for understanding and relevance for our lives, both personal and communal, we will seek out and share resources that challenge us to think, to ask questions, to value spiritual insight. Reflection can be prompted through many means – contemporary and ancient, familiar and unfamiliar – art, music, nature, literature, and humanitarian effort.

Because we have a vision of peace that cannot be brought about through violence and strength but only justice and compassion, the communities we seek to support and build need to strive to identify and resist injustice in all the places of hurt in the world. This includes de-humanizing and oppressive conditions, structures, attitudes, messages, and ideas, even when those structures, those ideas have been our own. We must work to create, recognize, celebrate and support conditions that enhance equity, preserve dignity and respect individuality.

The life of faith is seen as a journey comprised of ever-new experiences and understandings of self, others, the world, and the divine. Everyone is on their own journey. They will make their own choices of resources, discover their own pace, and hold their own understandings of things spiritual. And though there may be times when we believe we are alone, this is not so, for we journey together in the spirit of divine love.

The story of our faith is familiar.
It gives us the feeling of home;
each character, element, word
a welcome reminder of whence we have come.
Yet we feel the surge of curiosity
captivate us as we explore
beyond the tale we tell so well.

May our hearts be worthy of the quest for adventure.
May our minds be up to the challenge of the task.
And as life sifts us through yet another telling,
may we find in the newness of the tale
another home.
As we travel, might we remember:
we are not alone,
for we journey together
in the spirit of divine love. [2]

---

[2] Gretta Vosper, *Another Breath* (Toronto, File 14, 2009)

# The Resurrection of Whole-i-ness

*A segment of a reflection based on The Features of West Hill United Church, A Progressive Community of Faith in the Christian Tradition in celebration of the completion of that document. Prepared for and used in the gathering in Easter Sunday, 2004, and at subsequent CCPC events.*

All living things are hard-wired to keep life going—
to grow, reproduce, to seed, to re-grow,
life spending itself to recreate itself.
Life on this planet is incredibly diverse
and unbelievably beautiful.
From the frightfully powerful energy of viruses and bacteria,
through the sublime whorls of a nautilus,
from the peaceful unfolding biologics
of the plant world,
to the majesty of a breaching whale,
from the glee of mammalian jostling,
to the beauty and freedom
of that which can leave
the confines of the earth,
the world ever fascinates us.
It is just this that makes us human
—this fascination with the world,
with each other,
with those things we cannot even see, but only ponder.
It is this fascination that separates us
from creation in a marvelous and awesome way

and gives us cause to wonder.

In all ages, there have been two basic ways to view
civilization
—as a single communal organism
or as a collection of individuals.
Each has its own blessing and curse.
To see it as a single organism,
as it was seen in Jesus' day,
can create a society that encourages individuals
to seek the common good,
to go beyond their own personal satisfactions
to the satisfaction of the whole,
to work as a team.
At the same time, such a community
can devalue the variety of human life,
and value human life, itself, very little.
On the other hand,
the society that sees humanity as made up of individuals
can encourage each and every person to achieve their
potential,
or, it can develop systems that use the humanity of some
to provide advantage and privilege for those who have,
through whatever means,
achieved power.
In communities of whole-i-ness,
we seek to resurrect a world
in which all persons are seen to have inherent worth and
value.
We seek to create community
in which all are able and encouraged to seek meaning in
their lives
and to develop that which we would call their spiritual
nature.

18

We recognize that there are many ways in which this is
done,
many options for personal spiritual development to take
place,
some of which will not even involve the word "spiritual."
In this whole-i-ness community
each person's right to find their own way
is honored,
whether it involves ancient or contemporary rituals
or traditions,
religious or secular means, and we challenge ourselves
to be open to new understandings of the Divine
as they are made known to us.
Our scriptural heritage has contributed
to our understanding and development
of the spiritual values we cherish:
love, forgiveness, wisdom, nurture, and creativity.
We honor the divine presence within each person
and hold a deep reverence and respect for creation.
Jesus taught us that each person must take responsibility for
their life,
their choices and their spiritual growth
and to look deep beyond the ordinariness of life
to find within it that which is holy.
As those early communities that grew up
created a new kind of whole-i-ness power in the world,
so do we *choose* to be part of this community.
We do not attend because we have to
or because we should,
but because we see a radically different way
that the world might be
and in community,
we can be supported and encouraged
as we seek to live that out.

It is important to us that community be built on trust
honoring the contributions each individual
has to make to the whole.
The best decisions are those made
with the best information
discussed fully and respectfully
and with a desire to understand those
who bring diverse viewpoints
to the conversation.
When we fail, when we hurt,
when we experience brokenness
we seek mutual healing through forgiveness and love.
Our driving purpose is that all our actions
in all aspects of our lives
would reflect the divine, unconditional love we experience.
So
we try to live with compassion,  understanding, kindness,
and respect – helping, mending, healing and making whole -
to the best of our abilities.
Moved by sacred hope
and convinced of the profound significance of each person
as an infinitely precious being,
we dream and plan and implement positive change
to enhance the well-being of self, others, and the whole of
creation.
We embrace a vision of peace through social justice.
We strive to identify and resist injustices
in all the places of hurt in the world,
including de-humanizing and oppressive conditions,
structures, attitudes, messages, and ideas.
We strive to create, recognize, celebrate and support
those conditions that enhance equity, preserve dignity
and respect individuality.
The divine nature of the love we seek to share

moves us to recognize the sanctity of life.
We offer, invite, model, raise awareness and educate –
others and ourselves –
yet all the while honoring people's cultures
and respecting their freely made choices
which enhance life.
Living in a community that celebrates
the resurrection of Whole-i-ness
means we must look for understanding
and relevance for our lives,
both personal and communal
and so we actively engage with resources
that challenge our thinking,
encourage questions,
and offer spiritual insight.
Strong spiritual grounding
accompanied by healthy personal reflection,
evaluation,
and positive application
is important to us,
as it has always been to those
who seek to bring right relationship into being.
We are prompted to reflect through many means –
contemporary and ancient –
familiar and unfamiliar:
art, music, nature, literature, and humanitarian effort.
We see one another as primary sources for experiencing the
divine
and seek to develop ourselves for one another
and the community beyond.
We cherish this as a serious responsibility
and a joyful privilege,
calling for commitment,
humility, and lightheartedness.

The life of faith in a community of Whole-i-ness
is seen as a journey comprised of ever new experiences
and understandings of self, others,
the world, and the divine.
Finding meaning for ourselves
is our personal responsibility.
As we seek that meaning, we enjoy the freedom
to challenge all concepts
and develop our individual understanding of the divine
over the course of our lives.
Everyone is on his or her own journey.
They will make their own choices of resources,
discover their own pace,
and hold their own understandings of things spiritual.
And sometimes, it will seem as though
we are not moving forward at all.
But even then, there will be value in our experience.
We encourage each other to live authentically,
to strive to live to our full potential as responsible,
loving people,
while also embracing and dealing with the reality of our imperfections
and their impact on ourselves, others, and creation.
We are not alone in this life of faith, for we
journey together in the spirit of divine love.

# Re-genesis of the Corpus Christi's Corpus Callosum

*George Street United Church, Peterborough, ON, 2005*

I come to you as the spiritual leader of a typical United Church congregation. It is made up of men, women and children who range in age from infancy to 94. There are two-parent and single-parent families. There are couples and singles with and without children. There are individuals who have experienced the breakdown of long-term relationships and those who are planning ceremonies to commit to the neverendingness of their love in the coming year. There are truck drivers, musicians, artists, doctors, financial planners, counsellors, nurses, tons of teachers, principals, secretaries, homemakers, clergy and scientists. There are those who choose employment without remuneration and those who are seeking paid, accountable work. They are a congregation made up of people just like you.

I came to them, almost nine years ago, as a minister trained at a United Church theological college with two pastoral charge experiences of team ministry and some administrative Church House experience behind me. They were welcoming and loving and we fit together well.

It might have been the tall guy who sat on the left side of the sanctuary who first tipped me off to one subtle difference between this congregation and the others I knew and had served. He seemed innocent enough. A banker. Wore a suit pretty much every Sunday. His partner had been on the search committee. His kids were in the youth group. But every week, he'd make his way to his pew with a copy of Robert Funk's The Five Gospels: What Did Jesus Really Say? tucked under his arm.

Now The Five Gospels, for those of you who are not familiar with it, is a book written by the Jesus Seminar that is the compilation of all their decisions about whether Jesus really said the things he is recorded as having said. Red, pink, grey and black beads are used by its fellows to vote on each passage. Red means he said it, black means he didn't and the others are somewhere in between.

Each week's selected lectionary passages offered up one gospel passage and my copy of The Five Gospels told me that very few of them, as in two, were really voted on with total favour by the Jesus seminar. So as the weeks passed, I found myself reading the Hebrew Scripture lection very closely, eager to find an opportunity to preach on it thereby mitigating the possibility that I'd be caught preaching on something the revered fellows had decided Jesus never actually said.

This man, sitting in a pew every Sunday morning, thumbing purposefully through The Five Gospels, was no doubt oblivious to the fact that he was the incarnation of a major shift that had been happening in that congregation for almost 20 years. The re-genesis of the corpus christi's corpus callosum.

The corpus callosum, for those of you who are not anatomy experts, is that broad, thick band that runs between the right and left lobes of the brain. The left lobe is the place where language resides. It is home to analytical thought, controls what happens on the right side of the body and is generally believed to be the place where our rational thinking works itself out. The right side of the brain, connected to the left side of the body, is more creative, intuitive, less rigid. It is where our artistic abilities grow and develop. The corpus callosum transfers information between the two hemispheres.

During some gestation periods, the corpus callosum does not develop properly or at all. In other situations, to treat devastating, medication-resistant epilepsy, it is actually surgically severed, usually nowadays, in part, rather than completely.

And that, in a nutshell, is what I think may have happened down through the ages in the church, the body of Christ, the corpus christi,: what would usually connect both sides of the brain didn't develop or was, at some point, severed.

## Theological Training

How on earth is this relevant?

Let me go back to my training as a United Church minister.

While at theological college, students focused on the two major aspects of leadership in the church: the academic and the practice of ministry.

An enormous amount of our time and energy was put into the academic aspects: We studied languages (Hebrew and Greek); the Bible which included various methods of biblical criticism; systematic theology; and church history. I thrilled with it. It was as though the left side of my brain had been starved for this stuff. It was stretched, kneaded, pulled apart and, for the most part stitched back together again. For some of us, it was a pretty traumatic experience—bits and pieces of our previous belief systems were entirely excised and replaced with ideas that were utterly new. Indeed, we were, mostly, introduced to a Bible we had never read, a church tradition we did not know and the complexities of theological thought that demanded mental calisthenics previously unexhibited. It was a challenging time, academically.

Concurrently, in classes about worship, and the sacraments, we were taught to see, smell, taste, and touch the holy in the world of liturgical arts. Most of what I had ever seen up to that point in the few congregations I'd known had been pretty straightforward, United Church stuff. In the mid-80s, the whole world opened up. We could dress up in different colors each with a different significance, light candles, sing and sway at the same time, even express ourselves in dance if we felt like it, connecting ourselves, all the while with the most ancient traditions of the church. Communion bread was soft and torn right in front of us, the crusty little day old bread cubes of our Methodist heritage (or was that a Presbyterian thing?) were a thing of the past. We were awash in the sensual experience of the holy, lamenting the days wasted in the "Word" when there was so much "sacrament" to be celebrated, so much to see and do. We learned the art of worship. We were introduced to a God that could be experienced. A banquet of sensual delights had been set before the right sides of our brains and we gorged ourselves on them. Every single quivering synapse fired in rapturous delight. It was a nourishing time, liturgically.

So we were developing both sides of our brains at the same time, nourishing them with the latest in scholarship (left side) and the depth and beauty of the aesthetic tradition of worship (right side). You can see where I'm going with this.

What was missing from the theological education that I received, and many others with me, was anything that actually connected the two different things—the corpus callosum of the curriculum.

While we filled our left lobes with contemporary fodder, we stuffed the right with the mysteries of the past. Academically, we were offered up-to-the-minute biblical criticism, a perspective of church history that was blistering in its assessment of the activities of the early growing ecclesial powers and authorities. The Nag Hammadi and Dead Sea libraries were introduced as original options for or alternatives to the canon, as well as the writings of theologians that queried much of the traditional orthodox teachings of their predecessors, some of whom were silenced for their work. Liturgically, we steeped ourselves in the stuff of tradition, the language, the theology, the beliefs, the images that had been handed down through the beautiful tradition of the church. Worship was offered as an art form—academics as a tool for contemporary critique. Truly, the two could not meet.

Many of us have felt the absence of that corpus callosum throughout our ministries. We have congregants who ask us big questions. We run into old friends who stare at us in disbelief when we tell them what we're doing now. They can't believe we believe all that stuff we say on a Sunday morning and we can't answer them because, yeah, it's true, we say it.

## The appearance of normal

Now, you can't tell when someone has no corpus callosum unless you look very closely at their behavior. Most people look absolutely normal. But if you hold a card with a word on it out to their left, they won't be able to tell you what the word says. That's only accessible when it is seen by the right eye, not the left. As long as the right side of the brain is connected to the left, it doesn't need to know how to read the card; it can get its information in a couple of quick synaptic bursts of energy. When it is separated, though, it can't do that. What it can do, however, quite miraculously, it seems, is learn to read. In fact, it has been suggested that those who do not have an intact corpus callosum might, one day, be able to read two books at the same time, understanding each as well as the other!

I believe this little trick is how many of us have survived the split-brain theological dilemma in which we have found ourselves. We've made the creative, artistic side of our brains in which the beauty of the liturgy resides accommodate the parts that it couldn't understand. Rather than just staring blankly at the card with all the theological and biblical stuff on it that didn't make sense in the context of our ancient rituals and traditions, we began using metaphor as an interpretive tool. In a way, we taught the right sides of our brains to read. We use the creativity of our right lobes to interpret the demanding content of our left ones.

And we've done it very well. Over the course of a generation or two, most of the membership in the United Church has become comfortable translating what is sung, said, and read on Sunday mornings through the use of metaphor into something palatable. For the most part, congregants happily deny the virgin birth, but sing Silent Night, Holy Night without a problem; they repeat the words of the Kyrie, "Lord have mercy, Christ have mercy, Lord have mercy," and don't for a minute wonder about what that means; they end their prayers with "In Christ's or Jesus' name, Amen" without blinking about their own implied unworthiness before the face of God. Pick up the hymn book in your pew and turn to any hymn. Turn to another one. In far too great a majority of cases, the language has to be translated metaphorically for you not to wonder why you sing it.

New understandings of each theological word, each creedal statement, each hymn, each parable have developed over time and we have been translating for so long that we have become oblivious to it. We might say we need salvation, but what we mean is the job that will let our spirits soar, the mending of a rift in a familial relationship, the new perspective that will make us understand our place in the world. When we say "I believe" at the beginning of a creed, we can remember, as Marcus Borg has recently taught us, that it meant something different when it was first written and so it can mean something different for us now. Most of us, those of us who have been in the church for a long time, don't even know we're translating—we've taught the right side of our brains to read and it does the work for us.

There are, however, those who cannot make the metaphoric adjustment, who tire of translation, who do not understand why it is so important that we say one thing and mean another, who see no sacred purpose in words that place us face down in front of a God who needs to be appeased, who are offended by the language that has seemed so integral to our faith. They are uninterested in teaching the right sides of their brains to read. They do not want to have to learn the mysterious translations of an ancient theological code. They want "I believe" to mean the same thing on Sunday morning as it does when they're talking to their kids on Wednesday afternoon. They want to connect their need to experience and ponder the sacred with what they know about the world.

My banker, in his suit and tie, with his book tucked under his arm, is perfectly capable of seamlessly translating the words of favored hymns, but his act of bringing contemporary scholarship into the sanctuary became for me a symbol of the need to reconnect the two hemispheres of the theological tradition—for those for whom metaphor is not working. What contemporary scholarship has disclosed about Christianity, not much of which is very new at all, needs to be welcome in Christian worship spaces without the need for translation. There are those for whom the only meaningful language is that in which they normally converse. For them, we need to be able to talk about our faith without having to resort to words that need translation or explanation. Our work is with ordinary, everyday people and should be accessible to ordinary, everyday people.

The man with the book happens to be the same man who leads a book study at West Hill every year. This winter will see the cracking of the cover of its 21st book. Twenty years ago they looked at Tom Harpur's For Christ's Sake an exploration of the question of Jesus' divinity. It's been exposure and struggle, exposure and struggle ever since then; each book exposing them to some aspect of contemporary scholarship then requiring that they struggle with what its implications are for their belief systems. In essence, they were preparing the ground for the re-growth of the corpus callosum; Friday night they'd grapple with the concept of salvation not having any meaning for people who do not see themselves as innately sinful; Sunday morning, they'd sing Amazing Grace. Friday night they'd talk about how the Bible wasn't the literal word of God and on Sunday hear intoned after the scripture reading, "This is the word of the Lord. Thanks be to God." Friday night they'd talk about how the vengeful warlike Yahweh God served to displace matriarchal goddess religions and then on Sunday hear passages that stilled the sun in the heavens so that Yahweh's people could take another whack at their enemies. As the disconnect became more and more apparent, the need to create a path for information housed on one side of the brain to get to the other side grew more and more urgent.

Change began long before I arrived at West Hill. Awareness of the exclusivity of language altered the beginning of the Our Father in 1992, five years before I got there. The word of the Lord is no longer read; in its place we hear stories and readings that are the witness of God's people. Change keeps happening as the words we use are held up and scrutinized. Indeed, the "Witness of God's people" is currently on the list of things that needs to be reviewed—our understanding of ourselves as a select group, of God as a distinct being, are being questioned in the light of our current experiences. Almost two years ago, parents of church school children, recognizing that the Lord's prayer which was recited at the end of the children's time, even with its inclusive language Our Loving God, did not represent a vision of what they understood God to be. They requested that we change it, write a new one. It took me several months to get up the nerve to approach that change. But we did. And the prayer we wrote has become very important to our children. Some of you will already know it:

> As I live every day,
> I want to be a channel for peace.
> May I bring love where there is hatred
> And healing where there is hurt.
> Joy where there is sadness
> And hope where there is fear.
> I pray that I may always try
> To understand and comfort other people
> As well as seeking
> comfort and understanding from them.
> Wherever possible,
> may I choose to be a light in the darkness,
> a help in times of need, and a caring, honest friend,
> And may justice, kindness, and peace
> Flow from my heart forever,

Amen[3]

A few weeks ago I received a phone call from one of our mom's. She'd been having lunch with a friend whose child played with her daughter. Her friend had been telling her children about making a difference in the world, specifically about Stephen Lewis who was due to speak in Toronto within a week or so. While they talked, the friend decided to read to her children our children's prayer which the parent from West Hill had given her. At the end of it, her 8-year-old son told her that he knew that prayer. Surprised, she asked him how he knew it and he told her that his friend, Caley, the daughter of the woman with whom I was speaking, had told it to him, memorized, start to finish, in the playground one day. It has been a long time since the Nicaean Creed has been shared in a playground and, I would expect, a long time since the Lord's prayer was recited, out of interest, for another child to hear.

West Hill made some terrific strides growing a new corpus callosum and working to bring its emerging understandings of the Bible, church and God in line with its worship practices. A few years ago, the board at West Hill and I were eager to place a stake in the ground to mark how far we had come.

Before I continue, I must acknowledge that referring to where we have arrived as a place in front of where we were suggests that one place is ahead of the other. I chair the Canadian Centre for Progressive Christianity and have heard many times that its name is arrogant, suggesting that some are behind us in understanding. Progress means that there is a forward place and a backward place. I'm not going to pretend that is not so. The reality is that understanding is not grasped by everyone at the same time. We do not all evolve in our thought at the same pace. But the direction of theological evolution, as with any evolution, is progressive, not regressive. Within that evolution, thought about God must progress. For instance, it is

---

clear to me that we no longer need a warlike God. The concept holds us in a tribal perspective that threatens to destroy our world. It is evil and divisive, and continues to rule people's minds because they believe their sacred texts are the authoritative word of that God. It is clear to me that tribal mentalities will do us more harm than good. It is clear to me that much of our ritual is based in superstitious beliefs about what we need to do to curry that God's favor. And while they may remain as interesting and even spiritually inviting rituals, our seeing them realistically as tools and not superstitiously as sacraments is extremely important. It is our growth in understanding, not our regression that will allow us to break free of our fears. So I do speak of progress, of working hard to move forward, of the difficulty of examining our beliefs and challenging them to stand up to our experience in the world. When we do so, we find that we can no longer say that God is in control unless God is a very distant and perhaps perverse being who toys with our lives wantonly bringing cancer to young mothers, horrific genetic imbalances to yet-to-be-born children, and tsunamis, earthquakes, tornados and hurricanes to anyone at any time. To let go of the belief in that capricious God is a movement forward into a future in which we will love one another without distinction or prejudice. I do not apologize for that belief.

Back to the stake. (not that "burning at the stake" stake....) We at West Hill wanted to identify the point at which we had arrived in our spiritual journey as a community of faith. Its position could then be used to define us, to challenge us to move forward and keep us intentional about remaining true to what people had struggled to articulate about their faith up to that point. We could have written a Statement of Faith, outlining what aspects of Christian doctrine we had come to understand as essential and eliminating or negating those we didn't. But the discussion quickly pointed to the fact that whatever we wrote down would continue to act, as Statements of Faith do, not only as a defining document, but as a dividing document. While we wanted to be clear, we did not want to exclude people right off the bat.

It is interesting that The United Church of Canada is currently grappling with the process of writing a new Statement of Faith, without, it appears, considering the divisive nature of such a task. Well, they do not want to divide the church, so much of the language is oblique, and they do not want to sever the church from the Canadian Council of Churches, either, so much of the language is also traditional. But they have not taken into account that the document will continue to divide them from those who do not see God theistically, Jesus salvifically, or the Bible literally. But there are many people in the United Church who do see God non-salvifically have a non-salvific understanding of who Jesus was and who are absolute non-literalists when it comes to the Bible. I believe that to write a statement of faith that excludes these people at this point in time would be a very sad thing. People with progressive perspectives on faith would still like to see the church as a valid place in which they can continue to explore and live out their beliefs.

Perhaps the direction we took at West Hill would be a healing direction for the United Church. It would create room for a diversity of beliefs, while remaining strong about what those beliefs demand of us. Rather than create a Statement of Faith listing all our beliefs and disbeliefs, we followed the lead of the earliest Christian communities. They had grown up following the death of this strange middle eastern preacher attempting to live out what it was he had said to them. The understandings of that, of course, were diverse and led to many different kinds of communities. Some were ascetic communities that parted themselves from the world and others charitable communities whose members risked their social status, familial relationships and lives working with the sick and society's outcasts. All of them, though, were known as Christians by how they lived and the choices they made, not, as became the case shortly afterward, only by what we believed.

The document we created, known as VisionWorks II, is a significant piece of work. There is much that we believe written within the text of that document, but the word "believe" is not present at all. Dispensing with statements of doctrinal belief, it presents a document to which almost any situation could be taken and examined in the light of its clear call to reverence life. Of course there will always be circumstances where two ways of reverencing life compete—is it my life we're seeing as sacred or yours? Often the two will call me to differing choices. It is my responsibility to determine which of the choices I will take. And I make those choices as a Christian.

The VisionWorks II document rests upon our beliefs, but does not present them divisively. It presents them as a way of life that can be embraced, that will challenge, and that would be welcome in the worship centres of our church. It allows for what we know in the year 2005, about our faith, our church, our traditions, to be integrated into our worship life with integrity. In our language, in our music, in our liturgy. It allows for full transfer of information through the newly re-grown corpus callosum. We pray, not to a God who might change things, but within a community that holds us in prayer. We sing not of ancient, no longer held beliefs, but of that which inspires us to work at our relationships and get them as right as they can be. We worship not a remote, judgmental deity, but that which is worthy.

## What we do believe

Our VisionWorks II document rests upon beliefs that have evolved within the congregation over the past several years.

*We believe in the sanctity of life that is often experienced in ways that cannot be measured and that far outstrip what we can see and taste and touch. We believe that there is much in this world that challenges the sanctity of life and that it must be defied. We believe that to be very hard work and that it takes all the shoulders in a com-*

34

*munity to bear the burden of the responsibility. We be-
lieve our experience of the deep sacredness of life is dynamic and cannot be named.*

*We believe that the Bible is a human construction and it
is, therefore, full of both human promise and human error. We believe that no humanly constructed book can be
the authoritative word of God and that we, who recognize this, are responsible to challenge such claims and
behavior that suggests such claims, particularly where we
find it in our own church. We believe that some of the
stories of the activity of the divine in the world that are
collected in the Bible are rich with metaphor and meaning and can enrich our understanding of ourselves, each
other and creation. And we believe that much of what is
described in the Bible as the activity of God is destructive
of relationship and equality, that it is tribal and divisive,
that, despite the best attempts that the authors were
making to describe their experience of the divine, they
have created a legacy of judgment, horror and despair
and we no longer choose to burden ourselves with that
legacy. We believe it is wrong to call such words holy or
sacred.*

*We believe that some of the words attributed to a man
called Jesus, myth or reality, are words that can challenge
us to seek alternate ways to live together and break
down humanly-constructed barriers. And we believe that
some of the words attributed to that man are words that
can divide and destroy relationship, not just by the way
they are used, but by how they are recorded. We believe
that they describe a concept of hell that was very real to
that man but is no longer relevant to us. And we believe
that, too often, his words have been used to imprison
people in that hell, a place only the Bible and other religious texts continue to describe and make real in this*

*world. We believe that we have the right and responsibility to free ourselves of those concepts that are no longer meaningful and relevant for us because we do not believe that he was speaking as the only begotten Son of God, but as one who sought, as we do, to understand the sacred reality that he embraced and we call life.*

*We believe that all that is constructed upon the church's claim that the Bible is the authoritative word of God must be questioned because of the error of that claim. We believe that the church's creeds, doctrine, liturgy, ecclesiology, sacraments, hymns and theology are based on that claim. We believe they should be assessed for their ability to support our attempts to live in right relationship with ourselves, each other and the earth, honoring the sanctity of life as we each experience it. We believe that, though there are costs associated with such work and that much we have loved will be lost, that we must accept those costs, grieve openly, and, with love, caring and supporting one another, leave behind that which would encumber our work. We believe we are gifted to create new understandings, that they can be rich and meaningful. And we believe and these new understandings, too, must be questioned as time and experience lay hold of them.*

*We believe that there are many who have spoken of or through their sacred realities in ways that open us to our tasks of building right relationship and loving from the core of our being. We believe it is right and proper to nurture ourselves with their words, with our own words, with the ways that we and others see and know and celebrate the divine in our own lives.*

*We believe that we are light to the world, to ourselves, to each other and that the world and all its inhabitants can be light to us. We believe that our values will guide our choices and that our choices are the incarnation of our beliefs. We believe that because this is so, it is more important for us to struggle to develop solid values for ourselves and society in order that we can strengthen the reality of love in the world than it is for us to be conversant in ancient theological terms.*

*We believe that our experience of the sanctity of life is best expressed as and in love.*

*We are at a critical point in our history, not just as churches or a denomination or a faith, but as the world. How we learn to live together in that world can be and should be influenced by those who are spending their lives seeking to discern the wisdom of the times, the truth that must be exposed to the light, and the sacred realities that can nurture us into wholeness and call us to right relationship with ourselves, each other and the earth. My enduring hope is that we will work diligently to create loving, caring whole-i-ness communities in which one need learn no special words or practices, but is nurtured and strengthened in their commitment to right relationship. In the name of Love.*[4]

---

# Disentangling Ourselves from Dogma

*Progressions, 2005*

The project being undertaken by The United Church of Canada is a big one. The church's highest authoritative body, the General Council, at its 37th meeting, held in 2000, directed its Theology and Faith Committee to examine its Statement of Faith and do some work updating it. In the words of the General Council, they were to "produce the draft of a timely and contextual statement of faith, with a view to circulation throughout the whole church for study and response, while honoring the diversity of our church and acknowledging our place in a pluralistic world and in an ongoing and developing tradition of faith with interim reporting to the 38th General Council," which met in 2003.

That draft Statement of Faith has been circulating throughout the church in the second phase of the discussion process and the Theology and Faith Committee was receiving responses to it up until last month. The Committee hopes that this draft, or another quickly revised version, will be available for presentation to the 39th General Council as it meets next August.

The current Statement of Faith was approved in 1940 as the fifteen-year old denomination completed the updating of their Basis of Union. Even as it was formed as a union of the Presbyterian, Methodist and Congregationalist churches in Canada in 1925, the doctrinal statements within its founding documents were recognized to be in need of updating. Those who engaged in the undertaking, in the same spirit as those who now engage in it, saw their work as part of an unfolding of the story of faith for their particular generation and clearly stated that they were not producing an infallible document intended for all time. The articulation of the beliefs of the United Church has always been and continues to be a dynamic process.

## New words or new beliefs?

At a recent symposium on the draft Statement of Faith, however, there appeared to be disagreement around the direction given to the committee by the General Council on at least one very important point. Had the General Council's direction to produce a "timely and contextual statement of faith" meant the Committee was to work toward expressing the doctrinal positions stated in 1940 using contemporary, inclusive language and imagery, or was it to articulate new understandings of the Christian faith as it has developed within the United Church of Canada even if those new understandings proved to be inconsistent with our previously articulated doctrinal beliefs?

Presenters at the symposium were divided on the topic. One argued strongly that the language used in the draft Statement seriously compromised the lessons learned at the Council of Nicaea and articulated in the Nicene Creed; specifically, that Jesus was begotten, not created. His understanding of the task is certainly that the Committee was to update language, not theology. Others noted a deficiency, as the draft statement continued to image God exclusively in Trinitarian language; they spoke of a need for the broader experiences of the divine that are known in the church to be reflected in its documents. Clearly, their perspective on the committee's work was that it write in a manner that allowed for new doctrinal understandings.

In the past, it may have been that the development of doctrinal statements and other documents of the church was appropriately reserved for those educated in such matters. Theologians have wrestled with the stuff of the faith for millennia, seeking to put forward the best their minds could agree upon in order to assist the faithful as they made their way through life. The simple folk of the church did not have access to much of the scholarship (indeed, for over half the church's history, did not have access even to the document upon which the church was built, the Bible) and had to rely upon those trained in such things to expose and then expound upon the truths of the faith.

But we do not live in the past, nor can we, for it is no longer only those in ecclesial leadership that have access to scholarship and discussion about matters of faith. Contemporary culture exposes to any who would seek it information about anything in which they are interested. And many, it would seem, are interested in things of the spirit, issues of faith, and that which we call the divine.

## Progressive scholarship

The scholarship that is at the centre of the progressive movement is not new. It has been around for decades. If one includes the voices of the many who spoke from outside the church or were expelled by it, one could say it has been around for centuries. What has made it so critical for the church at this time, however, is that it has become, over the last twenty years, widely accessible and wildly popular. And that has made all the difference.

What the scholarship that has been made accessible to the general public by authors such as John Shelby Spong, Marcus Borg, Karen Armstrong, and John Dominic Crossan tells them is, simply put, that the Bible is a record of people's views about God and life and meaning; it is not the authoritative word of God. Beginning by simply juxtaposing its contradictory texts and identifying the many voices in which several of its books are written, then examining it for the remnants of bygone worldviews and critiquing it from the perspective of those who were condemned by it, over the decades we have discovered it to be the work of many individuals, each of whom was seeking to express how they experienced what they called God and each of whom was a product of his or her times and the prejudices of those times. "God," as a compilation, became the

40

champion of those prejudices, almost all of which were tribal in nature. As a book about that God's activities, the Bible is clearly comprehensive. As a book that was written by a divine being and that expresses the authoritative word about life for all time, under any sort of rigorous scrutiny, the Bible simply fails.

For many, dealing with this realization has not seemed an insurmountable problem; we have simply chosen to read the Bible as a literary document. I would warrant there are few of us trained at mainline theological colleges who continue to believe unflinchingly in the stories of snakes and forbidden fruit, plagues and parting waters, stone tablets engraved by God's hand and the giving over of land into the hands of the Israelites along with the requisite women and captured horses. Few consider the stories of the virgin birth, the loaves and fishes, walking on water and the condemning of whole herds of swine to be exact recitations of things that actually happened. And those of us who have led worship through all these years while holding a view of the Bible as a literary document, have developed a certain finesse with the printed word that has allowed us to think about it one way and read, sing, pray, and recite it in a completely different way. But thanks to Spong, Crossan and others like them we no longer have the privilege of such split lobe thinking. We have been caught. Those who have read their books, and embraced their findings will no longer let us get away with such duplicity.

So, basically, if we are going to deal with this situation with any sort of integrity, my bottom line is that the new Statement of Faith needs to say clearly, in language that is not so obscure as to be unintelligible, that the Bible is not "the word of God" but a human construction that can be both helpful and harmful, depending on the passages used. It's as simple as that. But I can't imagine the Committee is hearing that from everyone. It certainly wasn't the prevailing view at the Symposium.

A significant part of the church wants to keep things just the way they are, no matter what, evidence notwithstanding, while

41

another significant part of the church (together with the huge element that doesn't even come anymore because they saw through us a long time ago) thinks it's time to come clean. It would only be a miracle of biblical proportions that would bring the two sides together in agreement on what a new statement of faith should say.

## So, what do we do?

Perhaps what is needed is not a statement of faith. During this time of transition, (this is being generous, for the time of transition has been the last two generations, we've just been slow on the uptake) it might be that we need to step back from saying what we believe and, instead, state the values we can agree upon. The core spiritual values are much more substantial than the various dogmas people believe. It's just that, in order to express this, we're going to have to give up a whole lot of the theological language in which we have been couching our message of love and compassion for these past nineteen centuries. When we do that, we find that the language of everyday experience is just as powerful a tool in getting across this hugely important message. And while theological language can and does exclude many views, common, everyday language can include a variety of perspectives, including those of a traditional Christian perspective.

It would most certainly be that the table needed to bring together those who believe that striving to live in right relationship with oneself, others, and the whole of creation is an important, if not essential, value in life would be much larger than would that at which would sit those only who believe we must symbolize such work through the proper distribution of the sacraments. So, too, would be the table around which those who seek to live compassionately when compared with the table set for those who do so and "pass the peace of Christ." Similarly, consider those who name love as their highest ideal and compare their number to those who state that believing Jesus is the only incarnate Son of God allows one to truly come to know God. For that matter, bring together all who work for the good of humankind and all creation and stand them up against those who claim to know God at all. The one can only ever be a subset of the other.

What calls us together, what gives us common ground, are the values that we share. Dogma, by contrast, will forever divide us. The pattern of articulating our beliefs goes back to a time when we believed it essential, for the sake of our souls, that we get it right. It must be that we have evolved beyond such thinking. Naming our values and supporting and creating communities that seek to live by them, will lay for us a new foundation upon which we might begin the work of re-creating a just and holistic world in which love is known by all.

## Eight Points

The Eight Points that the Board of Directors of the Centre for Progressive Christianity have approved seek not to present dogma but to offer the opportunity for connection to many who, both inside and outside of the church, yearn to express their faith in language that is not contingent upon a particular agreed-upon theological understanding. As communities of faith begin welcoming progressive perspectives, questions, and images into their worship spaces, as members of study groups challenge themselves and each other to grow in spiritual integrity, and as individuals seek out and embrace new ways of living out in their everyday lives the sacred life-enhancing values they have identified as worthy, it is our hope that these eight points will provide support for their journeys.

*The 8 Points of the Canadian Centre for Progressive Christianity*

By calling ourselves progressive, we mean that we:
1. centre our faith on values that affirm the sacredness and interconnectedness of all life, the inherent and equal worth of all persons, and the supremacy of love expressed actively in our lives as compassion and social justice
2. engage in a search that has roots in our Christian heritage and traditions

3. embrace the freedom and responsibility to examine traditionally held Christian beliefs and practices, acknowledging the human construction of religion, and, in the light of conscience and contemporary learning, adjust our views and practices accordingly
4. draw from diverse sources of wisdom, regarding all as fallible human expressions open to our evaluation of their potential contribution to our individual and communal lives
5. find more meaning in the search for understanding than in the arrival at certainty, in the questions than the answers
6. encourage inclusive, non-discriminatory, non-hierarchical community where our common humanity is honored in a trusting atmosphere of mutual respect and support
7. promote forms of individual and community celebration, study, and prayer which use understandable, inclusive, non-dogmatic, value-based language by which people of religious, skeptical, or secular backgrounds may be nurtured and challenged
8. commit to journeying together, our ongoing growth characterized by honesty, integrity, openness, respect, intellectual rigor, courage, creativity, and balance

The church is at a critical point in its history. Rather than accept what some argue is its inevitable death, I pray that it might find strength in the opportunities for change which are currently presenting themselves. In a world that is far too quick to claim our allegiances for profit, it is vitally important that this institution, which has stood for so long in opposition to those forces, continue to provide its important leadership. The church has much yet to offer. Perhaps speaking about what we value will give it some respite from the challenging arguments that will and must eventually divide it, for those arguments must be heard and a stand taken against the continued presentation of a potentially harmful document, the Bible, as the definitive word about life for all time. Focusing on the values we share and the life that is inherent in them may allow us, even with opposing perspectives, to continue to shoulder together the work of contributing to the building up of love and compassion in the world.

# Prayer: The "As We Live Every Day"

*Progressions, 2005*

One of the most lasting and significant aspects of almost every faith tradition is that of prayer. The world engages in prayer that is private, public, silent, spoken, calm, and energetic. It is used to celebrate and soothe, intercede and heal, to focus our energies and thoughts, and to open us to new understandings. In every case, it is an act of aligning oneself with that which is believed to be both immanent and transcendent, both at one's centre and beyond the furthest boundaries of the universe – the sacred, the holy, the divine.

Often, tangible symbols and objects assist us in our efforts to engage in prayer. Perhaps most familiar to those in the west is the Roman Catholic Rosary and the images it brings to mind: the beads, strung together and worn smooth, sliding through fingers that seem to read the invisible messages each bead transmits; the heavy oversized rosary weighing down the folds of a nun's habit; the rhythmic blessing of its hoped-for protection swaying beneath the rear-view mirror.

In the east, prayer flags have been used for centuries around homes, monasteries, and mountains acting as offerings to those who have achieved enlightenment and as prayers that will bless all. As the winds tug at the flags and rush on past, they take with them the blessings that the prayers release, spreading them over creation as they continue on their way. The colours, too, fade as the flags release their prayers, evoking Buddha's teachings and calling individuals to lives of reflective, self-less living. As new flags are mounted alongside the old, they highlight the image of life moving on and being replaced by new life.

Lights, floating on rafts made from slices of banana tree trunks and decorated with flowers and leaves, are set onto the waterways of Thailand as thanksgivings to the Mother of the Waters. Similarly, each morning in India, worshippers gather on the shores of the Ganges to cleanse themselves and set prayer lights upon the holy waters in thanksgiving.

Recently, the labyrinth has been revitalized as a significant tool for meditation and prayer, the following of its circuitous path providing an opportunity to focus on a particular image or issue. Ancient energy techniques such as Reiki are believed to tap into life force energies that are only now being studied for their medical and healing benefits – how close this seems to come to our traditional understanding of prayer!

But for progressive Christians, many of whom struggle with the understandings of God that are normally conjured up by the concept of prayer, even talking about the subject becomes difficult. Even more awkward for many is the practice of prayer. It becomes increasingly complicated by the theological struggles that a progressive perspective demands. Too often, as our images of the divine shift and morph, prayer takes on a negative aura, becoming identified with things of faith that one is choosing to leave behind as no longer useful.

Yet those who regularly include prayer in their spiritual discipline seem to enjoy a sense of well-being, comfort, and strength regardless of the images of the sacred that they have developed. For the community with which I serve in ministry, prayer is one of the most important aspects of our spiritual life even though the images of God that are held by the members of that community are incredibly varied. Broadening an understanding of prayer can allow for its retention as a vibrant spiritual tool during what might otherwise be a difficult journey of faith. A little bit of history and some anthropology may help deepen our understanding and appreciation.

## How we've imaged God

Before we can really look at prayer, it is important to look at the broader world of religion in which it is such a major part. Religion is the communal acceptance of a particular perspective on how we can best relate to and understand the parts of life that can't be explained. Long ago, when our prehistoric ancestors first wondered over their existence and the meaning of "it all," they postulated a deity who oversaw all of creation. They saw that deity as responsible for the rain and the sun, for the fertility of the earth, for the good that comes in life and for the bad. So it became important to interact with the deity to soften the realities and ease the fears associated with the harsh experience of life. Perhaps someone, a sage, wise elder or medicine man, may have experimented with different ways of interacting with the deity and found some ways useful and helpful and others less so. Time slowly embedded the rituals that seemed to work in the religious life of the community. Prayer, in its many forms and within diverse traditions, is one of those rituals.

Traditional Christian prayer postulates the same kind of deity – one that is in control of the world, that is merciful and loving, but also judgmental and jealous. Such an understanding binds us to rituals and traditions that were created to appeal or appease – to ask for assistance or beg for mercy from that remote god. We say that the world, with its immovable natural laws, is often "cruel and heartless," recognizing as we say it that we desperately want a god that has a heart, that will watch over us, that will keep us safe. A theistic understanding presented in the Judeo-Christian scriptures proposes a god-being with the capacity to hear us, be moved, and respond; it is imbued with our human characteristics. And so, as Christians have lifted their prayers to give thanks or to petition for some kind of blessing, it has been to a god that would be moved in the same way we would be moved by such actions.

48

By way of example, imagine being asked to help someone in a manner that points out to you a significant need that you can address in a way that makes you feel good about yourself. Such a request moves you to respond with whatever you can do that would be helpful. When you are thanked for your actions, you feel even better and are often, as a result, more gracious with your time and belongings. If, however, the original request comes with a "bad attitude," with an "I deserve this, so do it" sort of demand, your response is probably less than generous. You're less likely to be moved by the request – less likely to respond with a feeling of well-being.

We have projected these same human characteristics upon God throughout the centuries – please God and you will know blessing; offend God and you will not.

Similarly, we postulate, often based on scripture, that the human characteristics of prejudice and judgment also lie at the core of God's being. When suffering occurs, as it always does, we look first for a reason or a purpose. Perhaps we find a flaw in the individual's personal life, in their faith, in their being, and we hang God's judgment on that. Or we find in their particular race, or gender, nationality, or sexuality a cause for that judgment and we find the heart of God conspicuously aligned with our own fears and explanations.

Whether we have been aware of it or not, for some time now, we have been examining that concept of God with this new set of lenses. Seen through such an anthropological perspective, it is clear how prayer developed as a source of great comfort in an unpredictable, often stormy life. If we think life is unpredictable now, how much more it must have seemed before we had any understanding of biology, bacteria, or baby-making, the weather or the tides! Our need for security in a chaotic world is understandable and enormous.

When we see how theistic concepts of god developed to help us cope with the random nature of pain, suffering and blessing, we recognize that such an image is just that – a humanly created image. Our attempts to define something we cannot possibly understand or adequately describe has and will always be subject to the limitations of our human, fallible minds. God, Spirit, the divine, must be acknowledged as being beyond our explanations or it becomes an idol, a mere tool in our struggle with reality.

It is important to note that by recognizing we have constructed an image of God that has existed for millennia we do not trivialize that undertaking. It may be that we would never have survived as a species without such an understanding. We needed, during our struggles with an environment that was more often hostile than not, a vision of a future for our children and ourselves that we believed might be possible. Our understanding of an all-powerful, all-knowing, all-loving God gave us a belief in that future. It may have been the only thing that gave us the strength to survive. Our capacity to create an image of the divine that gave us that sense of security is awesomely wonderful. It speaks of the creative strength of the human species and calls us to draw upon that same spirit and sense of wonder to continue to imagine ourselves into a sustainable future. But just as our forebears did not stop developing their concepts to match their understandings of life and themselves in it, we have the freedom and responsibility to continue developing, to leave behind concepts based on certain images of God, and embrace ones that reflect our present understandings.

*Okay, but what new images are there?*

For one woman, long before she had ever heard the term "progressive Christianity," prayer took on the face of those she knew were holding her and caring for her through that medium. Waiting for news of her husband's condition following a life-threatening medical trauma, she only had time to call one person – a woman from a book study group at her church. She asked her to let others in the congregation know about the situation and ask them to pray for her. As she waited, eyes closed in her own personal prayer, she felt one, then another, then many of her church family become present to her. It was as if each person, as they heard of the circumstances, joined her and blessed her and she knew that, regardless of the outcome, she would continue to know the blessing of the presence of those people.

In another situation, some years later, as prayer filled the mind of a man whose wife had experienced a similar medical trauma and as he settled his mind upon God, to whom he was praying, no traditional image arose as the recipient of his prayer. Rather, one by one, the faces of members of his church family crystallized before him and he had an epiphany experience, realizing as he prayed that he was, indeed, seeing the face of God, but that God resided within his friends and family, not in an ancient and distant image.

And, in other, still-desperate circumstances, a different woman purposefully set out to address her newly formed understanding of God. Willing herself to see God horizontally, rather than "up there," she was yet unprepared for the resulting strengthening she experienced as the images of her friends and family quickly came to her and galvanized her prayer. She speaks of the action of her prayer adding the power of their prayer to the situation, despite their not knowing of the circumstances about which she prayed or that she was doing it. She drew upon their strength and received what was, for her, a tangible response.

Dr. Jack Good, in a presentation to the Canadian Centre for Progressive Christianity at its conference, Barriers and Bridges – An Honest Wrestling with Faith, engaged delegates in a process of re-visioning God. Taking a critical scholarly approach to the Bible, church history and the development of the concepts of God that have tied us to a theistic image, Dr. Good helped participants realize that we do not live in a world that is safely and securely within the arms of a "personal chaplain to the earth." Far too much of reality belies that image and any concept we hold of the divine must not contain that type of limitation. We must also lay down a false sense of rescue and take up responsibility for what we formerly put on

God. We must recognize that there "is no safety net. It is we who must be the safety net for each other."

This perspective offers us a radically new understanding of prayer – a liberating, challenging, empowering one. Rather than beseeching God's mercy, we find we are called to be god in the world to each other. Using the word "god" as a verb, we offer it to the world as we love and forgive and seek right relationship. We find in Jesus' ministry an incarnation of god simply because in much of his recorded work, we see that drive to live out in his relationships all the goodness we associate with the divine: his challenges to the status quo, his recognition of brokenness, and his upholding of the oppressed. We see that same incarnation in any number of social justice heroes and spiritual leaders, but we see it in each other, too. When we live out the values of love, mercy, compassion and forgiveness, we, too, incarnate God. Or, in different terms, *when* we love, we experience and express our fullest humanity, that is, our divinity.

So our prayer begins to resemble our commitment, our binding of ourselves to the work of living out those values. We listen for the cares and concerns of others and feel ourselves turning with compassion toward them to offer love and reaching out in whatever ways we are able. We search our own lives for the places where we are in need of challenge and change and open ourselves to the perspective that living in community can offer. We are made aware of the many ways in which the world remains a hostile place and seek to offer ourselves, our time, our resources, our energy to soften the cost that living demands in the world's most depleted and hurting places. And we find, in ways mysterious to us, that we experience healing, renewed strength, and courage when we have engaged in prayer, both privately and communally.

Scientific research seems to vary on the efficacy of prayer. Continued conflicting results make emphatic statements on its power potentially embarrassing and, therefore, impractical. Initial work, much attributed to Larry Dossey, suggested that prayer had a positive effect on people even when happening unbeknownst to them and from a distance. Tom Harpur's book, *Prayer: The Hidden Fire*, was highly influenced by those and similar studies. More recent work by Harvard Medical School suggests otherwise, while the John Templeton Foundation and the Mind/Body Medical Institute continue to study the links between the brain and spirituality that may, one day, conclusively determine the truth about prayer.

We are invited to move into new understandings of the realm of mystery we have long called God. It dwells in our relationships, in the urgent call from within to live responsibly and respectfully with the earth, ourselves and each other, in the inner strength we know we draw on even when the person or thing that once gave us strength is no longer with us. Seeing injustice, we move to challenge it; beauty, we move to celebrate it. Seeing pain, we move to heal it; love and we move to embrace it.

Although we may never fully know the reasons why prayer seems to be such a powerful spiritual tool even beyond the simple petitionary equation of its beginnings, our experience convinces us to hold up those values that we once saw as characteristics of a divine being and to seek to live them out, to live god, through our spirits, throughout our own lives. To do so is to pray.

# What do YOU think?

*Lecture, First-St. Andrews, London, ON, November, 2006*

*Daring to Think Progressively in the Church*

Over the course of the past several years, a trend has been taking place within congregations and in the wider world that is managing to draw the attention of one of the world's oldest institutions. Perhaps the word "trend" suggests that it is something that is of raging interest to a few people caught up in those things and that, over time, it will settle down and perhaps even dissipate. But I believe that progressive thinking in the area of religion and the church, specifically, is a trend in the sense of a major shift in understanding, and one that will demand long-term, tectonic change within the church. The challenge that progressive thinking is making to the church is one that is here to stay ...like it or not.

*Where did we come from?*

The growth of such an understanding has been a slow growth that has now reached what might be called a critical mass. For centuries, theologians and philosophers, biologists, astronomers, and scientists, have been challenging the basic premises of Christianity. Generally, their ideas have been rebuffed by the church. Theologians as early as the author of the Gospel of Thomas, believed to be the oldest existing collection of the sayings of Jesus, have been dismissed as heretical by the ecclesial authorities. Some

54

received harsher treatment than the anonymity of being overlooked in the creation of the canon, the collection of books officially sanctioned by the church as the Bible, as the church burned, excommunicated, and tortured those who expressed perspectives out of keeping with ecclesial orthodox doctrine.

## Contemporary Scholarship

In the past 50 years or so, contemporary scholarship has found its way into theological colleges and, from there, in drips and drops, into congregations. For the most part, however, reactions to contemporary questioning of ecclesial doctrine have been harsh and only a few have been able to comfortably discuss progressive perspectives on church doctrine in their congregations. Then, more recently, in the last 20 years, contemporary liberal Christian scholarship made a leap from the seminary to the pew as books by John Shelby Spong, Karen Armstrong, Elaine Pagels, Marcus Borg, and Jack Miles, hit the mainline presses and began to be read, hungrily, by those who have never attended theological training centers. People began to be skeptical of what was being said from the pulpit, sung in the choir loft, and read from the lectern. The rumblings of tectonic shift had begun.

## The Center for Progressive Christianity

In the mid-90s, after thirty years of leadership in a congregation once referred to as the citadel of progressive Christian thought, Jim Adams acted upon his long-standing concern that congregations were not open enough to those who were sceptics. He started The Center for Progressive Christianity in the States with a $250,000 gift from an ardent supporter. His desire was to assist congregations as they made themselves more welcoming to those who were not willing to check their brains at the door on their way into church. Evidently, he had identified a very strong need in America and began, very quickly, to open Progressive Christian training centers across the country. His work has encouraged the development of similar networks in Great Britain, Ireland, France, Australia, New Zealand and here in Canada.

## The Canadian context

Here in Canada, when a small group of twenty-five gathered in January 2004 to discuss creating a network, the need was quickly apparent. Going around the room and learning why this diverse group of individuals had found it important enough to gather together to discuss this topic, we heard, over and over, of the isolation people were feeling in their congregations as leaders and lay members, and in their lives as they felt excluded from the church.

It was felt that the work that needed to be done in the Canadian context was different from that of the American context. There, the work was focused on making churches welcoming so that a sceptic would *want* to engage in the process of Christian initiation and indoctrination. We have undertaken to create a network of individuals and communities that were using and are willing to grow theologically *beyond* the ecclesial doctrines which are no longer relevant in today's world – there is no need for indoctrination. We want to make communities of faith that do not require anyone to learn anything other than the values upon which we believe much of our tradition is built.

Before we get started, I want to note who the audience to whom we are speaking is. There is no desire, as I hope I make clear, to tear someone's beliefs out of their hearts. On the contrary, if someone's belief system is working for him or her, helping them bring light into the world, then it can stay intact as long as it is doing so. If it's damaging other people, oppressing them, frightening them, or denying their inherent worth and dignity, then I'll get in the way, happily. So, who we are trying to speak to and for are *people who have stayed within or those who have left the church and those who were never there to begin with for whom Christian dogma, ritual, and traditional language does not work as a tool for spiritual growth and development.*

## A Progressive Perspective

What we have brought to this process is what we call a progressive perspective. Such a perspective can be applied to anything from education to nursing and health, to scientific research, to architecture, to gardening. Here are a few of the things that would make a perspective what we would call progressive.

There are four requirements for a progressive perspective to emerge as an idea: openness, passion, creativity, intellectual rigor. And there are another four that are necessary for a progressive perspective to emerge within any discipline and begin to manifest change: honesty, courage, respect, balance.

## Openness

If you wish to bring a progressive perspective to something you have to be open to new ideas, challenges, differences. Whatever your preconceived ideas are, you must become open to critique, to allow them to be added to by something else. As long as you are a teacher who believes that writing lines on the board is the only effective method of discipline, you're not opening yourself to new perspectives; yours is not progressive. Perhaps the most difficult part of being open is the need to lower our estimation of our currently held beliefs enough that we are receptive to others, to be non-arrogant about what we know so that we can hear what others are bringing to the table. An open perspective is non-defensive and encouraging, it is able to suspend judgment and to hold ideas tentatively as they are assessed. It will be comfortable with complexity and ambiguity, not needing to have all the answers all at once.

## Passion and Creativity

No new thought arises in any mind in any discipline if it's owner is not passionate about what they are doing or is unable to think outside of the box. Think about it. Limited liability laws. At a time when countries were reaching into new lands, developing new markets, learning about new technologies, the risks inherent in those things were huge. It would have been easy to be frightened away from investing in projects that involved such huge risk—ships sinking, wares going up in smoke, whatever. But someone was passionate enough about it that they created the limited liability laws that protected investors to the extent of their investment. So they could put money into a venture and not be afraid of losing their shirts on it. It took a passion for exploration and development to think progressively to a new way of seeing investment. Of course, limited liability laws are now used indiscriminately. It is going to take another passionate thinker to rewrite them in a way that can protect our world from the damage that many have wreaked upon it under the protection of those laws.

## Intellectual Rigour

New scholarship is available in every discipline by the minute. Physicians can hardly keep up with the latest developments in cancer prevention and treatment – but they have to try. Seeking out variety of scholarship from many viewpoints is essential to a progressive perspective. We want our physicians to be committed to deep, life-long study so that they will always have the best ability to diagnose our ailments or to treat them as they become understood. And these days, we want our physicians to be able to look beyond their drug-centered training to alternate fields of health and well-being. We want them to be able to be vigilant about their own prejudices so that they can bring us the best. We want our physicians to be progressive thinkers.

## Honesty

A progressive perspective is *honest*. Given the information that is available to you, you acknowledge that which you believe to be true and then choose to incorporate it into your perspective. You don't know that something is true and then choose to ignore it. In terms of insurance, for instance, you can't know that your insurance will not cover you for the use of your facility by outside groups and then decide you won't apply that knowledge to all your outside groups. You would be legally liable for not being honest in your use of the information you have at hand.

## Courage

In any discipline, progressive thinking is thinking outside the box and comes with a number of obvious detractors. There will be those who become vitriolic as their previous understandings are challenged. There will be those who are marginalized by new thinking. A member of my congregation, 94 years old, grew up in Saskatchewan as the automobile was coming into the fore. His father was a harness-maker whose whole livelihood disappeared in a few short years. Progressive thinkers need to be courageous not only in promoting truth as it is understood, but also in deciding where and when compromise is warranted; not only in confronting tradition but in receiving and *inviting* critique, in sustaining criticism and rejection.

## Respect

It is hard for us to think that someone is open to new ideas and discovering new terrain in their field if they are not courteous, humble, loving, or inviting. To think progressively one must hold an unconditional positive regard for all including those who do not hold a progressive perspective – one might have much to learn from them. A progressive thinker will hold the quest for truth more passionately than their ideas about it so they will be non-aggressive, holding back from forcing their ideas on others, non-coercive when speaking about them and non-derisive when hearing from others.

## Balance

The effect of progressive thinking on any discipline can be profound. Recognizing that means you need to move forward at an appropriately careful pace, seeking harmony, avoiding unnecessary extremes. This one is hard. Once you have the vision, the frustration you will feel as you try to achieve it will be great, but it is essential that progressive perspectives be presented with care and that they not be used as bulldozers.

*Applying a progressive perspective*
*(The following is the script for a slide presentation created to illuminate the efficacy of progressive thinking across various disciplines and compare the advancements made in those disciplines with the advances made in Christianity, or any other religion.)*

Progressive perspectives have been constantly applied throughout history. We're going to look at some of them and, just as you notice your niece or nephew's growth more dramatically when you've had a little time away from them, we're going to get a perspective from a little while back so that we can see the differences that progressive perspectives have made in a variety of disciplines.

Standing in to represent the 14th Century... a bishop from the south of France. And for the 21st century, the behemoth to whom everyone turns for the answer to any imaginable question, You-Know-Whoogle.[5]

We begin by asking about contemporary knowledge in the area of geography.

Our French bishop shows us a map of his known world and explains the areas off to the sides with a wave of his hand and the words "there be dragons".

---

[5] This is actually a Nudibranch-Hypselodoris Bennetti but I imagine that's where most of James Cameron's and Dr. Seuss' creatures came from: the sea!

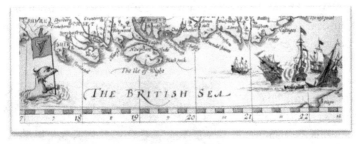

6

You-know-Whoogle, applying progressive perspectives that have culminated in six hundred years of discovery and map-making, shows how a map of the known world is really a picture of something that is quite round and quickly identifies North America, Antarctica, Hawaii, the Arctic, and the lack of dragons in any of the charted areas of the world.

[7]The Bishop, in answer to a question about the stars, explains that each of the heavenly bodies, as it moves across the heavens generates a particular musical note determined by the length of their orbit…. around the earth, that is, and that they make what is known as the music of the spheres.

[6] http://charleshahlen.com/wp-content/uploads/2014/06/flat-earth-map.jpg
[7] https://commons.wikimedia.org/wiki/File:World_map_indicating_tropics_and_subtropics.png

You-know-Whoogle, applying contemporary scholarship, goes into a long description of the various gravitational effects of the planets on each other as they rotate around the sun, the galaxy our solar system is in, other galaxies, the age of the universe as understood by calculations using the speed of light and the distance of galaxies on the edge of the known universe, etc.

Turning now to the field of medicine, the Bishop explains trepanation, the process of drilling a hole in the skull to cure epileptic seizures, mental disorders and, my particular ailment, migraines.

You-know-Whoogle tells us of several modern medical advances, including the little orange pill known as Eletriptan, which therapeutically eliminates my migraines and saves me the messy cleanup involved in regular trepanation. Of course, who knows? Maybe a single hole drilled in my head may have spared me years of agony and left me with only a scar that a little hair styling would have easily hidden.

Back to the Bishop, and on the topic of sex. (Sorry, no pictures of fourteenth century sex are available for download.) Ordinary people who choose not to devote their lives to ascetic observances are advised that their best defense against the ever-present urge to copulate is to marry early, preferably soon after reaching puberty. All sexual relations outside of marriage are sin. It is also sinful to have sex during menstruation, pregnancy or while a woman is nursing, during Lent, Advent, Easter Week or Whitsun Week (seven weeks later), on feast days, fast days, Sunday, Wednesday, Friday and Saturday, during daylight, when naked, or when in church. It is also forbidden unless you are trying to produce a child. (Take a moment to take that in....)

And to You-know-Whoogle (sorry, still no pictures) ...Well, let's just say that you don't want to do a search for sex and ever again be able to browse Facebook with your kids in the room. You-know-Whoogle provides you with way more information than you thought you'd ever need and still ends up landing you on the Babeland website. (You know you want to look that up...)

Our final topic is Christianity in the church and we turn to the Bishop who gives us the basic premises of the religion to which he belongs. The Bible is the authoritative word of God and the Church has been appointed its protector and keeper. Jesus is the Christ, the only begotten Son of God...Well to keep things short, he reads us the Apostles' Creed because, although there have been more modern creeds, like the 7th century Nicene rewrite, they are all so much longer so he reads, *"Credo in Deum Patrem omnipotentem; Creatorem coeli..."* Here's the translation: "I believe in God the Father Almighty, Maker of heaven and earth. And in Jesus Christ his only Son our Lord; who was conceived by the Holy Ghost, born of the Virgin Mary, suffered under Pontius Pilate, was crucified, dead, and buried; he descended into hell; the third day he rose again from the dead; he ascended into heaven, and sitteth on the right hand of God the Father Almighty; from thence he shall come to judge the quick and the dead. I believe in the Holy Ghost; the holy catholic Church; the communion of saints; the forgiveness of sins; the resurrection of the body; and the life everlasting. AMEN." A somewhat formal but succinct presentation of fourteenth century Christianity.

Now to You-know-Whoogle who is happy to respond, "What he said."

While there has been tremendous scholarship undertaken in the field of religion and religious studies, the stated doctrine within ecclesial institutions continues to reflect the beliefs of centuries gone by. The Apostles' Creed continues to be said on a weekly basis in many churches and its doctrine remains posted on the websites of many seemingly progressive denominations. We *appear* to have little progressive thinking happening in the church since the fourteenth century.

Beliefs in every other discipline have taken us far beyond what was known or understood in the fourteenth century. Almost anything the bishop told us on any other subject would be laughed at by any grade 4 student. But the church still teaches its children about virgin births and judgment, and resurrections of the body. Progressive thinking in the area of Christianity has been perfunctorily dismissed. It is time to change that. So, we bring our progressive perspective to the church.

## The Church's One Foundation

But, before we do that, we need to articulate what we mean by church. According to one heartily sung hymn, the church's one foundation is Jesus Christ her Lord. I beg to differ. "Jesus Christ her Lord" is supported by a foundation of his own. That foundation is the Bible. Underpinning every one of the basic premises of contemporary, or fourteenth century Christianity, is the foundational belief that the Bible is the authoritative word of God.

To different denominations that will, of course, mean different things. For some it is the inerrant word of God. For others it is merely the word of God, though I haven't quite got my finger on the difference there. For others it *contains* the word of God, giving a little wiggle room for interpretation.

In 1992, The United Church of Canada argued about just what the Bible was. Apparently, it was too divisive to say whether it was "a" foundational document or "the" foundational document, so the General Council, which preferred to sound like they didn't know their grammar rather than that they didn't know their doctrine, issued the statement that, "The Bible is foundational document."[8]

There has not yet been a Christian denomination that has clearly stated that the Bible is not the authoritative word of God for all time (TAWOGFAT). The United Church may have tried, but with the grammatical calisthenics, we certainly have not been clear. And so the Bible still stands as an authority upon which much of our belief is based.

We say that Jesus is the Christ, because Matthew's Gospel – in the Bible – tells us that Simon Peter said he was the Christ.

We say Jesus was born of a virgin because it says that in the Bible (it took some bad translation to do it, but it said it, anyway).

We say Jesus was crucified under Pontius Pilate because it says he was in the Bible.

We say Jesus rose on the third day because, even though it is a really weird counting of three days, it says "on the third day" in the Bible.

We believe there were three wise men for absolutely no straightforward reason at all because it *doesn't* actually say that in the Bible but we choose to believe it anyway...

*Doctrinal Development*

While there were many, many, many things that were said in the Bible, they were not sufficient to clarify all the questions that the early church had as it grew and so it held councils to determine just what the answers to those other questions were.

Over the course of time, many of those serious questions needed to be answered. Like the question about when Jesus actually *became* the Christ. Was it when he rose from the dead? Was it when

---

[8] In 2012, twenty years after the challenging discussion that failed to identify which article to use in reference to the Bible, things changed. In what I have termed a sleight of hand, the UCCan installed the Bible as the denomination's primary text and made its other statements of doctrine subordinate to it. Members of the denomination voted dramatically in favour of the shift because of the recognition of more modern statements *as well as* the antiquated Articles of Faith that appeared in the original Basis of Union. So relieved by the apparent updating of the doctrine, they neglected to realize that, in reality, they were going backwards.

he was baptized? Was it when he was born? Or when he was conceived? Was it before any of that, at the beginning of time? Bishop John Shelby Spong enjoys drawing that realization out for us, noting that, each of the gospel writers seemed to have a different understanding. (Funny how that eluded most of us.) In attempting to determine which one was correct, the Council of Nicaea chose to side with the Gospel of John. Jesus came into being as the Christ, with the Father from the beginning of time.

Similarly, the discussion about salvation was not clear at all so the early church put parameters around it, developing doctrine that explained it and sacraments that assured it. The result of all that doctrinal development is an extensive body of beliefs articulated in many different ways, some of which are incomprehensible to one who has not spent years in theological training. What it means comes into reality in the working life of the church – the things that the church does.

### Currently Articulated Beliefs

I would argue that the *articulated* or *official, orthodox* beliefs of any church are evident in how it worships. It is true that there are those who worship in congregations who do not share the beliefs that are embedded in its worship, but the worship life of a congregation, I believe, reflects what it believes. For instance, in a communion service, there may be those in an Anglican or Roman Catholic service who do not actually believe that the bread and the wine change in substance and become the body and blood of Christ. I don't know, I haven't asked anyone, I just think it's a possibility. But the words that are said, and the way that the elements are treated reflect the articulated beliefs of the Anglican and Roman Catholic churches. Sometimes, as in the ordination processes within The United Church of Canada, the rituals actually reflect beliefs that have since changed. The UCCan no longer holds that an ordinand's substance is changed through the act of ordination and that they are thereby "gifted" to approach God in a direct way. However, our ordination rituals continue to reflect that former understanding. So our worship life continues to hold the beliefs of our community of faith or retain elements that are no longer believed but are held onto for any number of reasons.

Generally, in our worship, we act in ways that continue to a) *elevate the Bible as the authoritative word of God*; b) *set individuals up as mediators of God's grace*; c) *dispense sacraments tied to salvation*; d) *pray to a remote God for our every need*, even when many people in the congregation and those in leadership may not believe in or uphold such beliefs.

## Applying Progressive Thinking to the Church

We want to apply a progressive perspective to the church and see what happens, going through each of the requirements that must be present for any change to take place.

### Openness, Passion, and Creativity

Allowing oneself the privilege of exploring the borders, setting the sails for the unknown and opening the mind for whatever might be found there can be as simple an undertaking as sliding a book off a library shelf and not closing it the first time it presents a new idea. Many have travelled uncharted territory in theology, liturgy, and ministry practice.

Some have left markings for us to follow. Passionate and creative minds have and continue to struggle with the unknowns found beyond the boundaries defined by the church. We have their guidebooks. Albert Schweitzer charted the quest for the historical Jesus and decided, in the end, that anyone who goes searching for Jesus, oddly finds a Jesus that looks just like the person on the quest. Paul Tillich set God free of the confines of a theistic "beingness" and drove us back to our own motivations and assertions to find the "god" we created there. Northrop Frye used his understanding of narrative and language to re-examine the Bible and belief and, in so doing, challenged us to allow our understanding of religion to be stretched by all sorts of cross-disciplinary studies.

## Intellectual Rigor

What Schweitzer, Tillich, and Frye brought along with their passion and creativity was an intellectual rigour that would not be distracted by hunches and undisciplined thought. They brought new insights that were strengthened by the study they undertook. Their work, and that of many others, contributed to the upsurge of contemporary scholarship that has been available to theological scholars for decades.

## Honesty and Courage

What was needed, then, to get the progressive perspectives of scholars out of the academy and into congregations, was the honesty and courage of the few who might risk their vocations to challenge the church to speak truthfully about the scholarship its leading theologians held as normative. In 1963, John A.T. Robinson, Church of England Bishop of Woolich in London, took that first step. *Honest to God* was met with astonishment, acclaim, and vibrant resistance and Robinson found himself in the midst of a whirlwind of controversy that has yet to settle. He died in 1983 without the satisfaction of knowing that his church had led the important work of teaching those in the pews contemporary scholarship and enriching their lives through the many means such scholarship allows.

With the works of so many progressive scholars and practitioners now on the shelves in libraries and bookstores around the world, it is no wonder that progressive thinking has become an important factor in the life of the church at this point in time. There is no other way to turn. The church has been, it would seem, trying to ignore its responsibility to think progressively. But the voices from within are growing and it must respond.

## Respect and Balance

First, however, we must be mindful of the other elements of a progressive perspective, because if we hope to have an impact on the church, it must be offered with *respect*. Deliberately, but with respect. And we must be keenly aware of the costs of that perspective. What are the people in the pews prepared to give up in order to move forward? What will they lose? How should the church best *balance* the forward-moving journey?

Let me set out what it is that progressive voices are presenting to the church based on contemporary scholarship currently acceptable in most liberal theological institutions.

We are asking that churches acknowledge the findings of scholarship that establish the human authorship of the Bible. By that, we mean that *any* claims that are said to be authoritative for all people for all time because they are of divine origin are really only of human origin and therefore:

- are no more authoritative than any other human statements
- are open to human critique

Additionally, biblical claims should be judged for whether or not they help us live together in right relationship and whether or not they adhere to life-enhancing values. If they do, we will lift them up and celebrate them. If they do not, they must find their way into the archives, Christianity's historical record, and no longer be treated as "holy scripture."

Progressive thinking in the church means that we have a lot of work to do. What are the implications of this clearing out of biblical claims that do not hold up to the rigor of progressive scholarship?

It means, as I just said, that we have to leave behind some things and embrace others.

Things to leave behind

First, some of the things we must let go of. I call them "constructions", because they have been constructed by the church, by our ancestors in the faith – mostly for what were then sound theological reasons, but that no longer apply.

We need to move beyond constructions that require adherence to supernaturally-sanctioned sources; that is, anything we have given credence to solely because it was presented as "the Word of God". With the authority of an external source undermined by serious study in theology, anthropology, history, and other major disciplines, we simply cannot accept what is presented as "the Word of God" as having implications for our lives without testing it through other means and purposes.

We need to move beyond constructions that require adherence to certain formulas, rituals, and confessions that claim efficacy beyond what an individual claims as her or his personal experience. For a long time, we have done things because we have believed they had a certain power if we did them in a particular way. For instance, baptism. Using the properly spoken Trinitarian formula assured that the individual is made a member of Christian society. One is admitted into that society when one is washed clean of sin by the process of Baptism. Although there is nothing biblical about infant baptism, our fear at the possibility that our children might be left out of that society ensured that, beyond the reformation, it would remain an integral part of many protestant traditions.

We need to move beyond the belief that we need the mediation of a particularly credentialed person to achieve spiritual growth. The role of the clergy in the church has been an exclusive role rooted in that ancient understanding to which I alluded earlier, that only those who had been particularly changed, could enter into the sacred holy places where God resided or was accessed. Only those ordained could enter the chancel area behind the screen that separated the sacred place from the "profane" in front of the gate places. But each person has the ability to connect with the sacred in his or her own way. We need to acknowledge the barriers we have created and allow all who would wish to participate fully in those things previously held as reserved for the clergy. In most Protestant churches, that means the elucidation of scripture, the power to baptize, perform marriages, and preside over communion. In the United Church, primarily presiding at communion, and baptizing.

Progressive thinking in the church means moving beyond constructions that use language that excludes on the basis of gender and sexual orientation. Well, we've been at this one for decades and we're still at it. Change is slow, I know.

The church needs, too, to move beyond language that is archaic, obscure, or specialized. I hold an opinion that differs from many on this issue, including the founders of The Center for Progressive Christianity in the United States and authors such as [the late] Marcus Borg who believe[d] we need only make our language palatable by using it metaphorically or giving it new definitions. I believe that the church must continue to be a force for change in the world. It must challenge systems that continue to oppress or imprison, even and especially when they are so subtle they seem invisible and even more when they are within its own institutions. The church has a responsibility to speak to significant issues of personal, communal, and global concern. It will, however, continue to marginalize and even silence its voice if it insists on reframing common realities in theological or biblical terms. Rather than requiring that those to and with whom we would speak learn our specialized language, it is time we began speaking our truths in the vernacular. Only then will we be heard on a scale that might make a difference in the world.

And finally, we must move beyond language that suggests sanction for unequal power relations between self and others, self and universe, self and divine. When we are saved and others aren't, when we speak of God as Thou and you as you, when we use words that continue to identify ourselves as chosen, we continue to fracture the human community and hold whatever good might come of our religious institutions at bay. This, I believe, is destructive. The church must move beyond this language.

## Costs inherent in Progressive Thinking

As with loss that is experienced in any organization, it is important to tally tangible costs. And there are many.

Following Tillich's lead and the work of dozens of theologians since, we find ourselves letting go of a theistic understanding of God. What does that look like? It hits home pretty squarely in the area of prayer and I hear of no other area that causes people more concern than the concept of prayer. What is happening if you aren't praying to someone who is going to do something for you? How do you reconcile the fact that so and so got what they wanted and you didn't? Or that you got what you wanted and so and so didn't. The reality is that we do not understand the whole of the world. We can't possibly understand it all. We, as a member of my congregation regularly reminds me, are babes in the universe. That doesn't mean that prayer does or doesn't work. It means I don't know and I'll warrant you don't either. It means that if prayer is a spiritual practice that makes you a better person, keep at it. It means that if you project your highest ideals outside of yourself, write them down and stick them up on the wall, use them to assess your life, your choices, your decisions, what you are doing is no different from praying as we have traditionally known it, to a God who we believed knew all. Pray. Pray incessantly, if you must. A theistic God may not work for me, but it may work very well for you. There is nothing wrong with an image. As long as we're honest about it being an image and don't presume to have better access or a more privileged place because of what we believe or how we manage those beliefs.

The second major theological shift is away from a salvific Jesus. It's been happening for a long time in mainline churches, but our practices don't look like it has. Those things that will most suffer from a progressive critique are the sacraments, those rituals and traditions that are clearly linked to the dispensation of salvation beyond this life. It is yet to be seen whether a symbol as strong as communion can be reclaimed with any integrity or if it will always be marred by the symbolism and doctrine that has rested upon it for so long.

And, coming full circle, we are back to the foundation, the centrality of scripture. A church that moves away from this very critical part of its history will look very different indeed. It will read from sources other than the Bible. It will file most of its hymns in the archives and be challenged to find new things to sing about. It will let go of its incessant need to analyze scripture, eventually being able to read it as Thomas Moore reads Poseidon or the story of Hercules – as a metaphor for life, an archetype that can deepen our understandings of ourselves. But that will take a long time, I am afraid. It will have to let go of the old Bible stories that it teaches its children, stories that have been etched on our hearts from when we were very young.

There will be much to lament.

## Things to Create and Embrace

It is not, however, entirely all about loss. Progressive thinking in the church means embracing new "constructs" while recognizing that these, too, are our creations; they are not dropped upon us from on high.

We can create new constructs that promote unmediated connections between individuals and the sacred. We all long for some kind of connection with reality that is so exquisite it is often called the divine. Through our experience, we find things that bring us that holy moment, into that place where we are silenced in awe. We might work on achieving such experiences or stumble into them completely by surprise. Each of us will find different things that do that holy work.

And, in my excitement, as I find something that works for me, I realize that it may work for you, too. I'll want to tell you about it. I might even want to show you or teach you how to do it. That is all very good. We need to teach each other the ways we find and speak of what is sacred[9] to us. They are holy practices. The most important thing, however, is that each of us searches, not that we all find the same way. The church can become a place that offers a variety of avenues to discover the sacred within oneself, in others or in the world. It can do this without telling us it is "the right way" to do it but rather as pointing us to a collection of resources it carries, tends, provides for our own exploration and edification.

As the church learns to do this, to be a resource instead of an authority, it will also learn to honor any inspirational, religious, Christian, or denominational traditions that underscore and facilitate such spiritual growth, with no additional requirements. Indeed, as it goes about that work, it will examine its own scriptures and those of others, philosophies, poetry and art and begin to honor all teaching on its merits alone. Nothing will be imposed because of "who said it" or "where it came from." If it is worthy, it will be retained and used; if it is unworthy, why would the church choose to keep it?

All of this is to lift up those things that celebrate, nurture, challenge and comfort individuals as they grow as spiritual beings and spiritual resources for the world. The responsibility of the church is no longer to get people into heaven. It is to grow spiritually healthy people who can act as spiritual resources in a broken and hostile world. This is no small commission and it may be essential to the sustainability of the earth and human life upon it.

Finally, as we learn to do all these things well, we will be called upon to support and develop initiatives that will help us to live out justice and compassion as spiritual values that are the essence of our work as Christians.

Celebrating

There will also be much to celebrate. As we seek out new things to teach our children, beginning, I hope, with a list of those

---

[9] I have begun the practice of defining what I mean when I use the word sacred. Now, if I use it in a lecture or in a personal conversation, I follow it immediately with words similar to these: "... by which I mean that which is so essential to our humanity that we cannot risk desecrating or losing it."

values that are so central to our survival and the earth's sustainability, we will create resources that will offer hope to many who currently see no hope in this world. It is often asked, what will be preached in our congregations? What will ground our moral decisions if we do not ground them in the bible (a questionable authority on moral decisions at any time)? What will we teach our children?

We will speak and teach about the values that we have distilled from the Christian message over the last couple of millennia. It's taken time for us to bear witness to them all, but here they are: love, forgiveness, compassion, humour, beauty, wonder, caring, delight, peace, truth, wisdom, justice, strength, courage, trustworthiness, joy, knowledge, fun, imagination, creativity, artistry, innocence, honor, tranquility, daring, purity, awe, challenge, respect, hope, and many more.

If we think of what the world would be like without one or another of these values, we find how truly important they are to us, how deeply rooted is our need for them. Imagine a world without trustworthiness; or a world without humour; or one with no compassion; or no courage. It doesn't take long to see how viscerally important these values are to us.

Inherent in a progressive approach is the ability to address these issues directly and to improve the relevance of the church's message. Because it is so important, far more important that what we thought we were doing before, it must be offered in language that is accessible to all. It will respect the intuitive faith that so many have felt well up from deep within them and honor the ways they seek to live out that faith, encouraging their growth and development as spiritual beings.

Ultimately, as we allow progressive thinking to influence our faith, making it as dynamic as it once was in the early years following the death of the one whose honorary name it bears, we will witness to the other faith traditions in the world that the values by which we live are values that are common to all. And we will call leaders in those faith traditions, and leaders who do not ascribe to a faith tradition at all, to a common table for the resolution of world issues. I hold this as my deepest, sustaining hope.

In the pursuit of that hope, I offer this new dynamic purpose to the church:

To become an institution concerned only with offering an approach to living that supports the development and celebration of right relationship with self, others, and the planet, and that helps us keep our values alive.

That is where I believe a progressive church can take us.

As the collection of our days
grows tall behind us,
our view of what might have been
looms large in its shadow.
We ponder over days gone by,
worrying our memories,
living's residue set upon our souls.
What has been, has been.
We can only move further away
from the choices we have made.
May the distance we cover
bring understanding.
May we grow wise
through the review
we make of our lives.
And, as our perspective widens,
may we find that our choices have been
part of a larger picture that, as a whole,
brings beauty to this fragile earth.

# In the Midst of Loss, a Season of Gift

*Progressions, December, 2006*

Christmas memories are deeply woven into each of our hearts. Whether the crinkled paper was on the floor in our own living room or strewn over that of a distant family relative, the heightened expectations, the sense of magic, the festive nature of the season, all these things made their way, for good or ill, into patterns by which we approach this season. They set our grown-up expectations and behaviors as we try to recapture moments imperfectly frozen in perfection or create the perfect moment that never was but for which we have always longed.

Growing up, Christmas consumed my world, not from the end of October, as it seems to do now, but certainly from the beginning of December. School concerts, Sunday School plays, impromptu skits and performances for my parents, everything revolved around the same theme. The stores bedecked themselves in lights and special displays. My siblings and I took our meagre pennies and purchased what we thought were the most beautiful things in the world for the most beautiful mother in the world.

Advent calendars weren't so popular back then. I don't recall even seeing one before I was an adult. Advent, itself, as a special preparatory period preceding Christmas, was unknown to me. There may have been lit candles in a wreath, but if so, it was something that was done without the participation of the laity – perhaps lit before the service and placed quietly at the distant end of the chancel, explanation seemingly unnecessary to its reverential task. Indeed, I don't remember special colors – the purple or blue of Advent, the white of Christmas, the green of ordinary days. All I remember is a green drape for the pulpit and lectern with, I think, a gold Alpha and Omega stitched on it, the mortar boards on the choir members' heads, and the folds of the ministers' academic gowns. If any of this changed with the liturgical seasons of the year, it was lost on me.

Christmas and its preceding few weeks, known as Advent, underwent major renovations in the United Church of Canada (UCC) over the past few decades. Much of it happened during the liturgical renewal movement that began in the early seventies and achieved a high in 2000 with the publication of the United Church's *Celebrating God's Presence*, a 700-page collection of prayers and services for use in congregations. Reflecting on the intellectual nature of much of the church's worship life, and possibly in conjunction with the conversations about union then taking place between the UCC and the Anglican Church, a swing toward a more sensual experience of God took place. It included the celebration of the different seasons of the church calendar along with their requisite color schemes, an increase in the celebration of communion and the use of the method of intinction (coming forward to receive communion by dipping bread into a common cup of juice, usually directly from the hands of the presider), the dramatic use of dance, candles, art, and music, responsive prayers and litanies, and an increase in the role of the minister as priest, one who "creates" access to the divine through their actions and words. All of these newer elements of worship have become common in the UCC in the last thirty years; few of them were common to our congregations before that time.

I can remember when we began going to church on Christmas Eve. It was a new thing for the congregation I grew up in and happened while I was at university – sometime between 1975 and 1978. The caroling family who annually entertained us at our front door having come and gone, we bundled up and filed through the backyard, crossing the street to the massive limestone church, windows glowing in the darkness.

It was wonderful. Garlands of ivy and wreaths hung from the balcony. The minister was in a long, trim alb, not the classic academic Geneva gown, a sign that something different was happening. We joined in with the choir as they led us through a Service of Lessons and Carols, something I don't remember ever experiencing before that night. For communion, we left our pews and each moved quietly down the centre aisle to take communion from the minister, joy streaming from his face as he gave us each the bread. I can't remember exactly whether we used little cups or not; what mattered was that it was the most holy moment I had ever experienced – exquisitely beautiful, reverent, rich.

And, of course, it was snowing when we came out. Or at least, I like to believe it was.

That midnight service became part of the pattern I now hold within me as sacred, despite the fact that it was new to me, not part of my tradition, not part of anything I knew before that night at all. The moment is remembered as being one of closeness with my family – mom, dad, sisters, brother, and everyone else in the church. It was expansive, connecting, real. Very real.

Christmas continues to change, to imprint new patterns of "holy" upon me. Moments of crystal laughter as a child tugs on the housecoat of Mary's newly-chosen Joseph, claiming her real paternity with total and utter innocence at one of our unscripted dress-up family Christmas Eve services. The depths of shared suffering felt as friends and strangers quietly position candles amidst the stars laid out on our Blue Christmas table, each candle a prayer for peace, healing, the end of ache, the resolution of discord. In the gentle light of those prayers, I have felt, and seen, hope return. My son, Isaac, and I travelling home, sometime after 1:00 on Christmas morning, in humbled silence having experienced a deep up-welling of awe as we walked a labyrinth together after the late service, sharing a little string of Christmas lights with those who walked with us, and standing together in the labyrinth's centre to watch the heavy clouds open overhead in a perfect little circle so the stars could blink down upon us. The sharing of light, flickers of hope in the darkness, spreading through the congregation as tapers bend and ignite, bend and ignite, person to person to person, joining us all together in a deep and rich connection. I pray that Christmas will always change in these glorious and holy ways, enriching me with its many treasures and delights and drawing new patterns upon my learning soul.

It may be that we have lost the innocence through which we once read the biblical Christmas stories. Indeed, the stories of a virgin birth, celestial signs, and heavenly choruses are understood now to be just that, stories. They were stories that were written to convince us of the divinity of Jesus, of his salvific power, of the deal God had made that would, finally, take sin away from us and from the world. We sing the purpose of those stories in all our old carols. We have known them from our birth and we love them.

When the carols no longer ring true, when we go to sing the words and they turn to dust on our lips, when we come to that place where we can only stare at the crèche and the camels and the star with utter dismay and disbelief, then, I believe, we are ready for the true power that Christmas can be. Then, and perhaps not a moment before, we are ready to hear a new song and find a way to share it with the world.

Christmas has been weaving its magic into something new for decades. It has changed before our very eyes, happening at about the same speed that attendance at church has been declining. One would think that, with belief in the original "reason for the season" dwindling, that Christmas, too, would end. After all, it is a religious tradition, clearly associated with Christianity—one would have to question why, in a postmodern world, those who didn't profess Christian beliefs would want to hold onto the tradition. Was it just for the two days of holiday? Was it just for the presents? Was it just because the kids liked Santa Claus so much? Aren't we, as many Christians have argued, at risk of losing the true meaning of Christmas?

Perhaps, but I don't think so. On the contrary, I believe we are just getting back to finding it.

Each of us is born into this world without any recollection of whence we came or understanding of into what we are being born. Life, in the moment of our birth, is pure, urgent, real, filled with potential. We are its instruments, whatever the vessel be in which it has arrived—male, female, black, white, ten fingers or no. We are also its clay, for from that moment on, life will work both upon us and through us. Within hours, it begins to imprint us with experience, teach us through our senses, mould us into who we will become. As we grow, we use what we know to affect and impact others and life is woven through the whole of our days into what we eventually and quite appropriately call "our" life, bruised and bruising as it has been.

At Christmas, we reach back and touch that innocence, that potential, that who-we-were-before-It-All-happened. We share stories that tell us of a holy birth and we resonate with the urgent simplicity we describe. We sing of awe and mystery and light and remember the wonder that new life is, remember the wonder that our *own* life is. Out of our stories, we can weave the mystery of life back into our hearts, make it well up and overflow, fill us with a sense of what is holy and perfect, and call us to celebrate that in ourselves, in every child's birth, in each moment of hope we encounter. In the season known for loss, we encounter stories of gift and we embrace them as holy. In the darkest days of the year, we find light and bask in it. In the Christmas that has unfolded outside our doors, we can find who we could have been and yet may be.

Taking leave of traditions that have grounded and held us is not an easy thing to do. May we be comforted in knowing that the core of what we have celebrated, the sense of overwhelming gift and love, no matter how the story has been told and interpreted, is with us still. We have but to open our hearts to it, walk into its midst and celebrate. In the depths of our knowing, we have not lost anything; rather, we find ourselves surrounded by love, by possibility, by what-might-be.

And this, above all, is the magic of Christmas.

# Merry Mmmphlgrb!! (???)

*Moving beyond politically correct seasonal greetings*

*Progressions, 2007*

It is probably the busiest few hours in retail – that mid-night-to-dawn transition that takes place once each year. With the echoes of the twelfth hour still ringing in the mall's clock shops, it begins. Hallowe'en is over and the stores begin their annual transformation. Black and orange decorations and unsold bags of candy are whisked with a magician's speed into some far corner of the establishment, and the boxes of Christmas trinkets, clothes, and toys begin spilling their contents onto shelves and into aisles and window displays across the whole of Christendom. Even the parking lot and main street lampposts are adorned while the relentless muzak of Christmas begins to take control of our minds.

*To everything there is a season....*

Each year, we're a little more disgusted at the speed with which the transformation takes place. Glimpses of preparedness were visible this year in the week leading up to that busiest of nights. Indeed, in some stores, seasonal colors clashed for the last few days of the month of October as red and green appeared prematurely on the same shelves as the purple-stockinged witches. Perhaps I'm just getting old and crotchety, but I do resonate with the ancient sentiment that holds "to everything, there is a season", that season should be respected.

And it is interesting that, even as the ghoulish creatures and the Snow Whites of Hallowe'en seem to turn ever more quickly into the tinsel and glitter of Christmas, sensitivities around Christmas are on the rise. Conically-shaped evergreen trees, laden with lights, decorations, and garlands, are renamed "Festival Trees" or, as one large store marketed them last year, "6-ft tall indoor air fresheners." Office personnel receive written policies outlining the appropriate manner in which to greet each other and the public and the manual from which that policy has been copied doesn't recognize the word that most obviously describes the season. "Christmas" is a no-no. "Holidays" are what we experience throughout November and December of each year. "Happy Holidays" if we are lucky.

*What's holiday about that?*

Holidays my foot. There is nothing holiday about the weeks between the snuffing of the last pumpkin candle and the rise of the earliest child on Christmas morning. Those of you who think there is have not yet prepared a "holiday" meal for a couple of dozen people, or wrapped packages until 4:30 in the morning, only to be shocked awake by the high-pitch screeches (apparently of delight) emanating from a 5-year-old an hour later. Or you've never had to navigate crowds in the mall when you've merely run out of dental floss or need a warmer pair of gloves. Or perhaps you've never tried to find seats on the train where you and a couple of wee children can actually sit together on the way home to your mom's for the "holiday." Or maybe you've never gone home for the "holiday" at all. Had you had any one of these experiences, you'd agree with me. There's nothing "holiday" about it. No. Nothing at all.

So what's the magic? Why do we do it? Why get all worked up about a festive season that seems to be more about marketing than anything else, that works its way to a fevered pitch you find still ringing in your ears weeks after it's over? What is it about this "holiday" that commits our hearts to it every year?

It's not Jesus. At least I don't think it's Jesus. Not the way the nativity scenes would have it, anyway. We know that Jesus wasn't born on December 25th, a date co-opted from those who worshipped the Sun and celebrated its birthday with feasts and orgies and non-stop partying. No record of Jesus' birth being celebrated on that date exists until the fourth century. So reverence for the date is merely misplaced.

And it's not about the details, either. We know that most of the elements of the two somewhat conflicting stories of his birth that we have, one from Matthew's gospel and one from Luke's, were embellishments laid over what could only have been a dearth of information, flourishes that, at the time, were common additions to the birth stories of individuals the community believed were great or blessed or even gods. From the star and its magi to the evil king, the killing of other babies, and the flight to safety, each element is a replication of some nameless but ancient story, some part of the hero archetype. We know they are not factually true.

## Things we now know get in the way

Those of us who have deep roots reaching back into the stories and festivities of Christmas associated with the Christian faith are challenged at this time of year. We find the things we now know getting in the way of the things we once believed and it mars our ability to embrace tradition, to sing beloved carols, to participate in rituals once held to be holy. We read signs demanding that Christ be put back into Christmas and we wonder what exactly is meant by "Christ," a word which is now used both by those who would understand it as a vast cosmic call to justice and those who understand it as a divine being who will reign as the final judge of all humanity. Two very different understandings. Two very different worlds.

Yet, even many who have explored the factuality of the Christmas story and who cringe at the materialism reinforced throughout the "holiday" find themselves captivated by the season. The pressing crowds in the malls would suggest Christians are not alone in that response to the bells and stars and glowing angels. Considering only about 20% of the population ever goes to *any* place of worship in any given week (that's Christians, Jews, Muslims, Buddhists, Jains, Zoroastrians, Hindus, Sikhs, etc., etc., etc.), but at least 90% of the population, most of which is *not* devoutly Christian, seems to want to elbow its way into the shopping courses of our nation each and every day throughout the whole of the "holidays," one would have to ponder the meaning of Christmas once again. It just can't be as simple as Jesus, too easily touted as "the reason for the season."

### Something much deeper

I imagine it is something much deeper than the story Christianity has claimed for the past two thousand years. Perhaps it was something rooted in that early solar festival church leaders recognized as holding such importance for the people. Perhaps (those who named it being northerners) it was in the dreadful fear of abandonment that primitive peoples experienced with the waning of the sun. Perhaps it was in the gentle pulse of life they celebrated as the daylight hours strengthened. Perhaps it was in the deeply-seated need they had to make sense of the inexplicable losses and gains experienced in their lives. Perhaps that movement of the sun, first away from them and then back again, catalyst for the creation of stories and myths, rituals and song, perhaps it acknowledged the fragility of life, their dependency upon things over which they had little control. And perhaps our realization of the tenuous hold we have upon life is ineradicably intertwined with this most mysterious of seasons.

Certainly that reverence for life would explain the hush that falls over us as we watch snow fall from a midnight sky, knowing full well that it is not a single sign humanity now seeks in the heavens, but signs of life, of intelligence anywhere else in this vast universe. It would explain the general feelings of goodwill so many experience, even and especially those indelibly marked with the realities and scars of individual lives gone awry. It would help us make sense of the influence Christmas as a holiday has in so many lives otherwise untouched by magic of any sort. It would give reason to the smiling faces that turn understandingly toward us in a long line-up or apologetically as bundles spill out from groping arms and land across our feet. It would allow us to understand more clearly the fear that grips the hearts of many at this time of year as they stare at the blank screens of their lives and wonder where the wonder went. And it would offer us, and them, a sense of beginning again, of renewal, of infant promise even, but this time, experiencing it in connection, deep, rich connection with all life spinning on this planet with us.

## The awe-full gift of life

It may be time for us to let go of the stated reason for the season and move on to a more inclusive recognition of the essence of our humanity and the "thread of life" we share with so much of what makes this planet beautiful. To do so will require, as all change does, a disentangling of ourselves from what we have known. It will require that we find new ways to image our deep connections, to shelter the fragile hope we are still challenged to offer a difficult and often angry world. It will mean trying to share our commitment to the values we name as sacred—love, peace, justice, compassion— with those who would be more comfortable creating fortresses of personal consumption and comfort, a challenging effort at the best of times. It will mean finding new ways to sing about, to speak about, and to honor the awe-full gift that life is, whatever the incarnation of it we happen to be living. And it will, very likely, mean finding something else to call it besides Christmas even though, for many of us, that word will continue to evoke images of new hope, new strength, new promise.

> Movement from darkness to light,
> from fear to community,
> from pain to healing,
> from loss to discovery.
> All of it part of a season we can say,

with renewed understanding,
brings light.

May we who ever seek it,
continue to find ways
to walk together within it.
Merry Wonderment.

# Dis-covery and Disruption

*Progressions, 2008*

*Every new truth which has ever been propounded has, for a time,
caused mischief; it has produced discomfort, and often unhappi-
ness, sometimes disturbing social and religious arrangements,
sometimes merely by the disruption of old and cherished associa-
tion of thoughts. It is only after a certain interval. . .that its good
effects preponderate; and the preponderance continues to increase,
until at length, the truth causes nothing but good. And if the
truth is very great as well as very new, the harm is serious. But,
at the outset there is always harm. Men (sic) are made uneasy;
they flinch. . . . [O]ld interests and old beliefs have been destroyed before new ones are created.*
*— Henry Thomas Buckle, English historian.*[10]

It was in his 1857 classic, *The History of Civilization*, that
Henry Buckle wrote these thoughtful words. They invite
us to pause, to consider those times when our own worldview has
been shaken and new understanding come to us accompanied by
the crash of former truths. And they challenge us to consider the
effect truths we bring to light will have upon those with whom we

---

[10] compiled from quotes in *The Making of United States International Economic Policy: Principles,
Problems, and Proposals for Reform.* Contributors: Stephen D. Cohen - author. Publisher: Praeger
Publishers. Place of Publication: Westport, CT. Publication Year: 2000. Page Number: 277.
*AND* William Bridges, *Managing Transitions; Making the Most of Change*, Addison Wesley, Reading,
Mass., 1991, Pg. 5

share a common cup of understanding. We are softened. Our desire to rush forward into the newness of what might be is chastened. For what we offer, filled with life and promise as it may be, will yet be experienced by many as utter loss.

Buckle is right. Old beliefs come apart and are destroyed before we ever have a thought that we might need new ones. Whether it has come upon us suddenly or over a period of time, as has the evolution of progressive Christianity, the acceptance of the new thought, the new idea, the new truth, alters our world in a blink. It doesn't come upon us gradually. Suddenly, we are without whatever system it was that formerly supported us and helped us to make sense of our world. Stripped of it, we experience change as a sharp, painful intrusion in our lives. Consider the vulnerable infant: if placed alone and unwrapped, fresh from the confines and safety of the womb, it almost instantly dissolves into a frantic, screeching paroxysm of distress, its limbs and fingers splayed, seeking the walls that once confined it and held it together. Its freedom is too new; its sanctuary too quickly lost. Comfort and security are replaced with the unknown before we ever have a chance of protecting ourselves from it.

We are like that infant; the world is new, the protection we have known in our religious systems no longer shelters us despite our anxious attempts to grasp it, wrap ourselves in it, and return to comfort. We sit in pews amidst the shards of former truths and our instincts are to piece them back together in a manner that will work for us, that will repair and return to us the calm and refuge we have lost. But we cannot. It would be so much paste and so little what we truly seek.

But we are not infants and we are not helpless. We know what it is that we must do. We have the ability to consider what we have learned, what we have lost, and what we want for the future. We can connect with one another and learn from each other. We can explore options and determine which work for us. We can project our ideas into the future and test their impact. We have the ability to create. We are not powerless. Indeed, our greatest anxiety seems to come from having discovered that power lies in our own hands. Much of the future will depend on what it is we choose to do with that power.

The process of creating the future is one that should take time. According to William Bridges, pre-eminent authority on change and managing change, how we make the transition from what has been, through the not-quite-there-yet space of Buckle's disturbing interval, to what is yet to be, is crucial in creating a sustainable and healthy future. Whether we are moving as a community or as individuals, our ability to separate, transition, and incorporate the new will determine the success of change.

Bridges builds upon the work of Dutch anthropologist Arnold van Gennep, who, early in the 20th century, studied tribal rituals acted out to acknowledging life transitions experienced by individuals and communities.[11] In each ritual, van Gennep found three phases. Whether moving from childhood to adulthood through a complex initiation rite or from one chief to another through a tribal ceremony, van Gennep noted differences inherent in each of the stages he identified. The individual or community acknowledged the ending of what was by creating a break or dislocation, moved into a period beyond the limits and expectations of convention and then, returning to the group or acknowledging new relationships, embraced the outcome that had been foreseen at the beginning of the process. Van Gennep called these phases separation, transition, and incorporation.

It would seem appropriate for the church and its trained leadership to take on the role of facilitating those transition rituals and in so doing, become a sort of midwife to change. We understand the cycles of life. We know how to celebrate beginnings and

---

[11] Arnold van Gennep, *The Rites of Passage*, trans. Monika B. Vizedom and Gabrielle L. Caffe (Chicago: University of Chicago, 1960; original 1908.)

91

endings. We can be pastoral in the midst of loss. We're good with ritual. It is a natural fit.

But there is a problem. The church, itself, is going through this one. It can't be its own midwife. As much as the role of mid-wife would suit it, the process is one with which the church, itself, needs assistance. Getting from where we've been to where we're going is not a simple, step-by-step process. It is going to be mucky. The harm, as Buckle says, will be serious. What we have known in the past – a strong, committed, relevant church – and what we want to be in the future – a strong, committed, relevant community of faith – is remarkably similar but the questions we have and must put to the purpose of such a body – why? and what? and how? – have nudged the church, bit by bit, away from its former firm foothold in society. And we have, finally, hit that stark moment of recognition: the old world is gone and the new one has not yet come to be. Aware of it or not, the church has skidded into van Gennep's "neutral zone," that place between leaving what was known and arriving at what will be. It, we, will need all the strength, vision, and fortitude we can muster.

Bridges opens his book *Managing Transitions* with a warning tone. "It isn't the changes that do you in, it's the transitions. Change is not the same as transition. *Change* is situational: the new site, the new box, the new team roles, the new policy. *Transition* is the psychological process people go through to come to terms with the new situation. Change is external, transition is internal."[12]

Nowhere would such a warning be more apt than in the "neutral zone" that exists between the solidity of the church of our memories and the amorphous vision of the church of our future. For van Gennep, we should remember, neutral also meant chaos. But we should also remember that chaos, with the exception of its use as the name of the organization of evil on the old TV show *Get Smart*, can be a good thing. It can be a place of potentiality, of nas-

---

[12] William Bridges, *Managing Transitions; Making the Most of Change*, Addison Wesley, Reading, Mass., 1991. Pg. 3.

cent promise, of what might be. With exceptional accuracy, van Gennep, decades ago, named our current space.

So it is especially important for us to be tuned to the possibilities of this space in which we currently sojourn. Like the metaphoric sojourn of the Israelites in the wilderness, we must take time to set our tents, hammering our pegs in firmly so that we make it troublesome to move too quickly. If we don't attend to the opportunities inherent in this chaos time, Bridges warns us, we might inadvertently destroy what it is we so want to create.

If we bolt, turn around, return to what we knew, we bring ourselves back into what has been a safe place but it will only be temporary. In reverting to the old, we would not only cripple whatever opportunity exists for a strong, committed, and relevant church, we would secure the final demise of the liberal and progressive church, a situation already fast unfolding. If we move too quickly forward, pulling our tent pegs and whistling our way to the future, we risk losing creative opportunities that can only gestate over time in the chaos of our no-home. Or we might choose to keep our tent pegs in our pockets, skip the wilderness sojourn altogether, secure ourselves quickly and immediately in the new place. There, acutely sensitive to its discomforts and challenges, not recognizing that discomfort is normal, it will be all too easy to convince ourselves that we were wrong, that we should never have attempted the journey. And so it is that we must set out our tents in this unfamiliar place, let them flap in the winds of change for a time, and be attentive to the mysterious mix of what was, is, and yet may be.

*Reaction*

We've already identified many of the things contemporary worldviews require that the church leaves behind. Now we have to acknowledge that loss, finding ways to do so that honor what it is we have left while making space for the new to grow and develop.

The experiences that we have of loss are personal and vary greatly. What some find as unshackling and exciting, others experience with fear and trepidation. Moving a congregation through tectonic change requires sensitivity. Those who want to move forward with haste, who are eager to pull up pegs and move into new unknown territory, must be celebrated and encouraged even as those who find security and comfort in the things of the past must be honored and cared for as the terrain becomes unfamiliar.

Bridges points out, as does Buckle, the reason we are in transition: things stopped working. It is important to remember that. The liberal church, as an institution, is failing, its belief system undermined by truths modernity has unfolded in its presence and that stand irrefutable before it. That is a hard fact, but a fact nonetheless. No single person, no single congregation, no single moment in time is responsible for that reality. It is the way things are. Many a theological student, many a layperson, many a congregational leader has railed long and laboriously in lament at that reality. Their caterwauling changed nothing. The fact remains—what once worked simply no longer does.

Acknowledging the failure of our belief system to sustain us is the first step in our transition process. That failure is so common, one would think it would be easy. It hits us in the face almost daily. Our prayers are unanswered, God's absence in our lives is palpable in the mess we make of them, the confessions we make bring no relief from our burdens, people we love get sick and die. The world continues to crack and fissure along the lines of entrenched religion. Instead of peace, we see war. Instead of having the promises of our religious heritage fulfilled, we continue in conflict with those who have alternative promises embedded in theirs. As it turns out, however, even with never-ending examples pointing to the failure of our belief systems, letting go of the system that has sheltered us from the angst of the cosmic neighborhood is no easy task. We hang on with temerity, refusing to compromise the faith that has been handed to us. We take our disappointments stoically, tuck them away, and face the world with the same naive belief that, next time, the system will hold. Each Sunday, that expectation is reinforced with platitudes and promises and it is easy to slip through life with a fuzzy idea of what it is that is really holding us up.

When we begin the process of bringing what we believe into focus, a destabilization begins. But it happens slowly and almost without note. As with all new discoveries, there is often a great eagerness to absorb as much as possible in as little time as possible. People eagerly dig up the roots of one's faith tradition, finding out who did what, and why, and the connection those things of old have with the things of now. Dismantling the belief system is an almost natural and comfortable part of that process as seekers peel away layer after layer of theology, ecclesiology, and Christology, to reveal the primal human instincts that sought meaning and led to the birth of religious systems and traditions. While there is much conversation and affirmation, the work proceeds with little conflict, little disagreement, almost in a harmony of purpose. All are attentive to the tasks of *dis*-covery.

At some point, though, those who have been about the task, who have been absorbed in the work, look up and look around. While so intent on it, they haven't noticed that the rain has begun to fall upon them, the wind to rustle their hair. They have been oblivious when the earth shook with the weight of giant, hand-hewn stones, crashing down upon it. When they finally look up, their work complete, or almost so, it is a devastated landscape that meets their eyes. Lying about them is the detritus of what was once their holy, sacred home. Its roof has crumbled, its walls fallen, the floorboards used for kindling, and the foundations washed away. There is nothing left.

This moment does not come all at once in a community of faith. Rather, it comes to one person and then to another, and another. Displaced and disoriented, people begin to see one another as those who sojourn together in an unfamiliar place, a place without markings, with no guidelines or maps, with no structure that can yet withstand a new system. While they set up camp, they remember it was they, themselves, who took their world apart. Or they begin to point fingers at those who led them to this devastation. Like the Israelites, they rail against the one who called them out of their comfort zones. They want to go back. But there is no going back.

On many occasions, individuals with whom I have worked who have otherwise engaged entirely in the process of *dis*-covering the roots of their faith tradition, right through to the acceptance of the human roots of the Bible, the impetus toward faith, even the concept of God, have, upon catching a glimpse of the seared landscape, reacted with deep and venomous anger. They know, intellectually, that they have discovered what is true, but they do not want to accept the implications of that truth. It means losing the safety net they believed was there, even though it had never been of any real assistance to them in their lives. Their sense of betrayal is enormous. It is important that they be offered tools that can help them assimilate their new realities and point them toward a place of wholeness and healing.

## Support

There are many ways to offer and find support. The situation, as we can readily see, is a pastoral one. It is one of bereavement. The loss individuals experience is very real. All the pastoral resources one would normally direct toward an individual who has been bereaved would be appropriate here. Rituals recognizing the conclusion of the former reality or counselling focused on acknowledging the loss and moving toward healing would be helpful. A series based on Bridges' Transitions book can be enormously instrumental in helping people move through the difficult terrain of no man's land. Support groups can be enormously effective as those who have experienced common loss find ways to hold each other. Often, as one speaks words of support to another who has been similarly bereaved, her or his own healing begins, the words spoken crafting a reality previously thought impossible.

The situation is perhaps more difficult when the person responsible for pastoral care is also the person who has played a significant role in the dismantling of the traditional Christian story. Yet that is exactly who they are most likely to be. Clergy trained in liberal theological institutions have been carrying the tools for deconstruction for a long, long time. They know how the Bible was written, the church formed, and the clergy set up as intermediaries for the divine. Perhaps the venom with which they are met when they use those tools is the reason the tools have stayed out in the back shed all these years.

It is important that denominational structures begin to put into place processes that ensure "safe passage" for those who are beginning to oil the tools and make them serviceable. Too often more ready to clamp disciplinary procedures on their clergy, denominations almost mandate their own demise by allowing those who have not been educated in contemporary scholarship to avoid being unsettled or challenged in their theological understandings. Without the support of their peers and overseers, clergy are rarely able to remain in a congregation long enough to bring about substantive theological change.

In the same way a university offers tenure to professors that allows them to do provocative research that may not otherwise be in the university's best interest, so, perhaps, it is time for denominations to create programs that protect the right of clergy to present congregations with contemporary scholarship within guidelines that assure pastoral responsibility. At present, there is no process, place, committee, or ecclesial court that identifies or takes responsibility for ensuring progressive thought is a significant element within the church. Without it, however, those who have already ventured into no man's land will starve for lack of resources and support, those who watch from the security of the previous paradigm will be well warned to stay put, and a viable future for the church will never be achieved.

Liberal denominations that take up the challenge of protecting their progressive clergy will find that they have an enormous wealth of passion and energy, are eager to be about transformative work within their congregations. Pastoral leaders can be trained and

97

ready to offer their care to individuals within their congregations who are experiencing pain. Groups such as the Alban Institute have been creating resources designed to help them move their communities through change and the conflict that so often comes with it. Protected from the threat of dismissal or disciplinary procedures, such clergy will be able to reach out to one another to find the collegial support they need to move forward, sharing their personal faith journeys, enormously reducing the isolation they have been forced to live within. The church, under their leadership, will move forward.

It is an exciting road we are on. The future has the potential to be incredibly rich and the church has the opportunity to be one of its wise and skillful guides. May we find ways to move into it that weave confidence and trust into the fabric of church leadership so that it, in turn, might weave confidence and trust into the reality that unfolds.

# Beyond God:
## The Next Inclusive Language Debate

*More Franchises, a Conference of The United Church of Canada,*
*2008*

*1 Corinthians 14:6, 9 - 12*

*Now, brothers and sisters, if I come to you and speak in tongues, what good will I be to you, unless I bring you some revelation or knowledge or prophecy or word of instruction?...So it is with you. Unless you speak intelligible words with your tongue, how will anyone know what you are saying? You will just be speaking into the air. Undoubtedly, there are all sorts of languages in the world, yet none of them is without meaning. If then I do not grasp the meaning of what someone is saying, I am a foreigner to the speaker, and he or she is a foreigner to me. So it is with you. Since you are eager to have spiritual gifts, try to excel in gifts that build up the church.*

*For this reason anyone who speaks in a tongue should pray that he may interpret what he says. For if I pray in a tongue, my spirit prays, but my mind is unfruitful. So what shall I do? I will pray with my spirit, but I will also pray with my mind; I will sing with my spirit, but I will also sing with my mind. If you are praising God with your spirit, how can any who finds themselves among those who do not understand say "Amen" to your thanksgiving, since they do not know what you are saying? You may be giving thanks well enough, but they are not edified.*

*I thank God that I speak in tongues more than all of you. But in the church I would rather speak five intelligible words to instruct others than ten thousand words in a tongue.*[13]

It may well be that Paul was referring to an ecstatic spiritual experience that has nothing to do with the traditional liberal preacher's craft, but his words provide basic rules of engagement for those who seek to lead in the church. If you're going to say something, it is hardly worth your effort if you do not make certain that you are being understood.

Language is a very powerful tool. We use it, as Paul suggests, to get information across, to teach, and to edify or build up those to whom we are speaking. We use it to establish a commonality of understanding and perception as in "That's a table" or "That's a chair", although in such instances the power of language to describe is greatly enhanced by our ability to augment the verbal depiction of it in a variety of sensory ways. See, hear, touch, smell, taste. By reinforcing our language with other sensory input regarding an object, we come to know it more completely and can more readily arrive at a shared understanding of it.

An example: while "A dining room table" might conjure up certain images for you, "My mom's dining room table" will mean little, if anything, to you. If I do not describe it, chances are your own mom's dining room table will loom before you or you'll project onto me some image of a dining room table that you think "suits" me. Until I describe it in much further detail or you are invited to join my parents for dinner and get your own first-hand experience of it, you will not know what it looks like, how big it is, whether it is stone or marble, or glass or wood. Only once I have described it can I say "My mom's dining room table" and you have anything more than a vague idea of what it is about which I am talking.

My mom's dining room table – solid mahogany, oval, a wide classic skirt, and carved tapered legs that are each about 8 or 9

---

[13] New International Version

inches wide. It's at least 4 and a half feet across and has enough leaves to extend it to over 21 feet in length. It smells of furniture polish and is burnished to a rich darkness that has deepened over its 120-year long life. When you pull your chair up to it, the depth of the skirt keeps you from crossing your legs unless, of course, you're where one of the leaves has been fitted. They don't have skirts on them. It takes three or four people to pull it open to add or remove the leaves. Every dent or scratch has added to its beauty – the marks of a family that believed eating together was one of its most important rituals and sharing the table with others one of our most important responsibilities.

Have a better picture now?

Language can unite us by placing before us a simple way to refer to things we hold in common without all the descriptive words that might otherwise be needed. The easiest things to describe are nouns – people, places, things – but because we have different experiences of them, such as my experiences of my mom's dining room table, even with the addition of several adjectives we can never really confirm that we are in perfect understanding with one another.

Of course, adjectives are a bit of a problem in and of themselves. Think of beige. We recently had our house trim painted beige. We chose the color from about 140 different shades of beige and we're still not sure we have the right one. Think of fast. How fast is fast? It depends where I'm trying to get and how important my meeting is. Slow? How slow is too slow? If we're talking traffic on the highway – 80 kilometers an hour can really tick me off. If we're talking a quiet afternoon with my husband and a thunderstorm, slow had better be way slower than that.

Beyond concrete I-can-see-touch-taste-hear-or-smell-it nouns, there are some things that no amount of describing is going to make clear. Think of pain. Or love. Or fear. We each experience these things differently—sometimes VERY differently. We can, perhaps, say what these things do to someone and get closer to a common understanding that way, but our experiences are, necessarily, going to differ. Pain is what makes you writhe and groan in agony but what makes you do that may be very different from what makes me do that. Love will make you give up almost anything in order to pursue it but it might cause you to give up far more or far less than I. Fear is tricky because it can either make you freeze or make you move – the classic fight or flight dilemma.

I expect you know where I'm going. If we have these difficulties trying to speak about things with any real clarity even if we consider them common objects or common human experiences, how much more difficult it is for us to speak about the things of faith? Understandings of God, of Jesus, of the spiritual quest, were we able to get the breadth of their diversity into our heads, would stretch the human mind to incredible proportions. We simply can't use a word and expect people to know exactly what we mean when we say it. At least, not any more.

When The United Church of Canada was formed, it was a lot easier. The Basis of Union, despite its being hammered together from three different denominational perspectives, managed to articulate a fairly concise definition of God. From *The Manual*, Section 2.1

> *We believe in the one only living and true God, a Spirit, infinite, eternal, and unchangeable, in His being and perfections; the Lord Almighty, who is love, most just in all His ways, most glorious in holiness, unsearchable in wisdom, plenteous in mercy, full of compassion, and abundant in goodness and truth. We worship Him in the unity of the Godhead and the mystery of the Holy Trinity, the Father, the Son, and the Holy Spirit, three persons of the same substance, equal in power and glory.[14]*

---

[14] "Twenty Articles of Doctrine (1925)," UCCan, http://www.united-church.ca/community-faith/welcome-united-church-canada/twenty-articles-doctrine-1925 Accessed, 28/08/2017

Even so, before the dust had settled on the newly formed denomination, work was underway to update the Basis of Union and, after several years wrestling with emerging theological constructs, a new definition was established in the Statement of Faith in 1940:

> *We believe in God, the eternal personal Spirit, Creator and Upholder of all things.*
> *We believe that God, as sovereign Lord exalted above the world, orders and overrules all things in it to the accomplishment of His holy, wise, and good purposes.*
> *We believe that God made man to love and serve Him; that He cares for him as a righteous and compassionate Father; and that nothing can either quench His love or finally defeat His gracious purpose for man.*
> *So we acknowledge God as Creator, Upholder, and Sovereign Lord of all things, and the righteous and loving Father of men.[15]*

Gone was the idea of an infinite, eternal, unchangeable and perfect deity; the Trinity found itself in a whole new section; and a clarification of God's dominion, extended to all things in all the world, was introduced. Perhaps it was because in the intervening fifteen years, as the understanding of God had been challenged, defended and refined, what had been assumed in the writing of the Basis of Union, had to be specifically identified in the new Statement of Faith.

By the time the print had dried on the new Statement of Faith, understandings of God were already needing to shift and change again. The second Great War, the pitting of Christian nations against one another, was cause enough for a great rewriting of theological tomes. How could God, appealed to with equal passion

---

[15] "A Statement of Faith (19400," UCCan, http://www.united-church.ca/community-faith/welcome-united-church-canada/statement-faith-1940, accessed 28/08/17

on both sides, not haul one team off the field in preference of the other? More critically, if our theologies supported the operation of gas chambers and the annihilation of a people, which they seemed to, did we not have to go back to those theologies and have another look at them? The disgust with which we now interpret the Holocaust was not quite so immediate nor assumed by the people of a faith who had just affirmed that the "Cross is for all time the effectual means of reconciling the world unto God." The realities of war challenged us to reconsider some of the "truths" we had previously so easily espoused. We had to go back and rethink the idea of God – what it meant, what it was capable of, what Christianity and its exclusive doctrine of salvation called us to.

Paul Tillich was one of the theologians who undertook that reimagining with vigor. German in his background, he accepted a position in New York after being dismissed from his Frankfurt teaching post in the early thirties – the result of the contradiction between his thought and the rise of Nazism. Tillich went back to the concept of God and reframed it, finding the extrapolation of the idea rooted in what he called our "ultimate concern".

Now, that's a pretty big leap. To go from an understanding of God as a being, a sovereign Lord over the entire world, to an understanding of God as our ultimate concern, a vague understanding of the "ground of our being" is a stretch to say the least. Indeed, Tillich's ideas, many of which are said to be expounded in his sermons in a clearer form than in his other writings, remained more than just a stretch for many – they weren't even on the radar of most believers. It wasn't until John Robinson, then Bishop of Woolwich in London, wrote his brief book, *Honest to God*, that the ideas Tillich put forward were able to make the leap from pulpit to pew.

Let me explain. When I read Tillich, I can barely grasp some of the concepts. The language, precise and educated as it is, has me in a fog almost from the word go. It takes a considerable effort to come to understand what he is saying and I almost always find myself having to go to a secondary source to get a grasp on his ideas. For the most part, theologians, students, and ecclesial officials were the ones who struggled away at the works of those who, like Tillich, were seeking to come to terms with the realities of a new world and the fractured doctrinal beliefs that had allowed, if not led to, the atrocities the world had witnessed. Most Christians, after the war, were building their families and their fortunes, looking for simple moral direction and an established social matrix, and trying to find their place in a society bent on appearing homogenous. They weren't, for the most part, reading Tillich and they weren't struggling with new definitions for God.

It may be that John Robinson didn't really make much of a dent, either. His book, *Honest to God*, was published in 1963 and meant to bring the scholarship from those on the edge of Christian theology, like Tillich, to the people in the pews. In it, intuitive understandings of God that had grown out of the dissonance created by the juxtaposition of reality and Christian doctrine were affirmed in more accessible terms. It immediately found its way into the hearts and back pockets of many students of theology. I regularly hear of the immensely freeing and affirming influence the book had on the lives of those who read it back in the 1960s, but never once has that news come from someone who was not ordained at one point in their lives.

In the late 1960s, the United Church presented a brief piece to be used liturgically as an affirmation of faith. It was clear from the beginning that the Statement of Faith from 1940 was never meant to be a liturgical element – it is long and unwieldy. Its purpose was purely to define, as statements of faith are wont to do, the parameters within which one could, with conviction, call oneself a Christian. Reciting the Apostles' or Nicene Creed as affirmations of faith had begun to grate against some of that more radical contemporary scholarship and required one's assent to doctrinal beliefs that had already been removed from the more contemporary 1940 Statement of Faith. The virgin birth, for example, didn't appear in that statement, an omission that was pointed out when more recent discussion over the 2006 "A Song of Faith" became heated in regard to that doctrinal tidbit. Even Tillich had only referred to the "virgin-birth symbol."

But both the Apostles' and the Nicene Creeds required believing that Jesus was born of the Virgin Mary, a theological stumbling point for many new thinkers in the United Church and those being educated with the most contemporary of scholarship in its theological institutions. And so, the United Church undertook to create this more palatable affirmation of faith and "A Contemporary Expression of Christian Faith" was written and accepted by the church in 1968.

Never meant to be creed or to replace the United Church's Statement of Faith but to be used as an affirmation, the piece gained a certain prestige when it appeared in the 1971 *Hymn Book* with the title "A New Creed." Accepted worldwide as a more palatable articulation of the basic Christian beliefs of the moderate or liberal church, it has appeared in the collections of many denominations since that time.

Despite the church professing that "A New Creed" was not a creed at all, it has been embraced by the last two generations of United Church members as exactly that. The image of God presented within it, however, in no way reflects the image set forth in the 1940 statement. Here we have a God who creates but isn't yet finished with creation; a God who came to be with us and remains present to us; a God who, no matter what happens – even things outside that God's control – will remain with us.

Gone from "A New Creed" is the exalted Lord who "orders and overrules all things in [the world] to the accomplishment of His holy, wise, and good purposes." Gone is the statement that humanity was made by that God to love and serve him. Gone is the image of Father. Gone is the sense of trust that God has a plan for us that nothing will defeat. Gone, along with all that, was much of the dissonance that the war and human atrocities had woven into

106

our clean and simple theologies of the past. It was a new world and a new understanding of God was needed for it. We needed a God we could trust to be with us even in the midst of ethical complexities and, in "A New Creed", we found one.

But perhaps those in the church who so love the words of this beautifully inclusive new God wouldn't recognize or remember it in its original version.

> Man is not alone, he lives in God's world.
> We believe in God:
> Who has come in the true Man, Jesus,
> to reconcile and make new
> who works in us and others by the Spirit.
> We trust Him.
> He calls us to be his church:
> to celebrate his presence
> to love and serve others,
> to seek justice and resist evil,
> to proclaim Jesus, Crucified and risen,
> our judge and our hope.
> In life, in death, in life beyond death, God is with us.
> We are not alone.
> Thanks be to God.[16]

In 1980, "A New Creed" was revised to make it more gender-inclusive. It was early on in what has come to be known as the inclusive language debate. By the time I hit theological college in 1987, that was in full swing.

As contemporary society began struggling with the implications of its overuse of masculine pronouns and images, a challenge brought to it rather abruptly by the feminist movement in the 1960s, it was natural that focus would eventually turn again to the concept

---

[16] Kevin N. Flatt, *After Evangelicalism: The Sixties and the United Church of Canada*, (Montreal: McGill-Queen's University Press, 2013)

of God. Scholars had long recognized that the idea of God was not gender-related, despite its being constantly identified as such in our foundational document, the Bible, and theological students had been exposed to a variety of ways of understanding the concept for decades. But feminist theologians noted that, even so, those who explored, wrote about, and presented theological constructs did so in almost exclusively male imagery. It was time for a change.

As in all disciplines, change in the core group of scholars can sometimes take years to get to the people on the street. Whether in education, medicine, biology, astrophysics, or theology, new ideas are ever-so-slowly processed to the point that they can be assimilated by those not steeped in the profession or discipline out of which the ideas are arising. It's as though they are being processed through the many stomachs of a cow, each attempt breaking the ideas down into more and more digestible bits and pieces until those who have no specialized language can finally accept and embrace the implications of the ideas.

With inclusive language, the idea was to get to a non-gender specific understanding of God, to open the concept up so that people could recognize, understand, and embrace an idea of God that resonated with their particular life experiences. If we were to follow the digestive process, we'd start with the iconoclastic ideas of Mary Daly who published *Beyond God the Father* in 1968 (the same year the UCC accepted the gender-exclusive version of "A New Creed"); process them through the work of scholars like Elizabeth Schussler Fiorenza, who showed in her 1978 book *God and the Rhetoric of Sexuality,* that she cared little for the gastric upset she caused her colleagues; refine them with the more accessible challenges of Naomi Goldenberg's 1980 *The Changing of the Gods* and Rosemary Radford Reuther's *Sexism and God-talk: Toward a Feminist Theology* (1983); or ingest a final purgative in the form of Phyllis Trible's graphic *Texts of Terror: Feminist Readings of Biblical Narratives* (1984). One way or another, the concept of God, without gender, was going to make its way into our consciousness.

One of the ways that the issue of gender-inclusivity was introduced in regard to the concept of God in the United Church was through an images workshop. Pictures of a variety of different things – people, nature, candles, spider's webs – were posted or strewn around a room. Workshop participants, at the beginning of the program, were invited to roam the room and choose a picture that most represented the image of God for them. When all had done so, they were invited to turn to one another and describe their picture and through it, their understanding of God. Scriptural metaphors for God would then be introduced – rock (Ps 18:2), fortress (Ps 18:2), light (Ps 27:1), moth (Hosea 5:12) – followed by female images – mother bird (Ruth 2:12), she-bear (Hosea 13:8), midwife (Ps 22:9) – and, perhaps, further scriptural allusions to God as mother – Deuteronomy 32:18: "You deserted the Rock, who bore you. You forgot the God who gave you birth"; Isaiah 63:13: "As a mother comforts her child, so will I comfort you" or the more graphic depiction of mother-love, Hosea 13:8: "Like a bear robbed of her cubs, I will attack them and rip them open." Slowly, ever so slowly, so slowly, in fact, that many congregations have still not experienced the shift, the recognition that the concept of God was open for definition spread across the church. With it went the understanding that any attempt to describe God could and should include a multitude of images.

While most redefinitions of God were undertaken in the subdued cloisters of ecclesial offices or the soundless studies of academics and only afterward made palatable and easily digestible for the laity by theology's practitioners, the clergy, this new redefinition began to happen right on the front lines. Emerging within the idea that definitions of God should be broadly inclusive, the freedom and responsibility to create their own definitions was not only taken up by academics and ecclesial officials, it was, for perhaps the first time, taken up by clergy as well. Responsible to create liturgies that evoked and provoked a broad understanding of God, and forced to think beyond the words traditionally used to address, define, and represent God, clergy, many of whom were women, introduced a myriad of new words, images, and liturgical elements. It was a subtle but profound shift of responsibility and, in terms of who had the authority to define God, it was an outright coup.

As the work unfolded, an interesting aspect of our creative process emerged. Apparently, when we neutered God, we not only removed gender, but, as so often happens when testosterone levels are radically reduced, we created a kinder, gentler being – the kind of God we in the liberal church have always wanted to have. With the shift of God from primarily masculine imagery, we inadvertently, I believe, eliminated many of the stereotypically-male traits that had infused our understanding of God up until that point.

Describing a male God, we often include words like warring, vengeful, angry, judgmental. Indeed, the Bible is rife with descriptions of a jealous, punishing, impetuous, and capricious God who consumes his people with his anger, sets upon their enemies with vengeance, dashing children against rocks, and ham-stringing horses; a God who answers those who anger him with plagues of vermin or disease, and either starvation or piles of rotting quail.

Even before gender-inclusive language, though, we had rarely begun our prayers with the invocation of "Killing God" or "O Vengeful One of Unspent Wrath." Calling on the somewhat more acceptable and well-loved image of a Father God seemed to have risen to prevalence in the liberal church. But that image, too, brought conflicting responses to the fore, encompassing as it did not only the idea of the loving dad who was always "there for you" in some way, but the Father who was never really pleased, who was always disappointed, who punished, who limited freedoms, who, no matter what our age, was always bigger and smarter and "righter".

So it was that liturgical practitioners distilled the understanding of God through the gender-inclusive language controversy to its most inclusive definition yet – one that lifted up the characteristics of love, compassion, forgiveness, strength, and comfort and left behind most of what had been held by former generations as

110

the one true God – no wrath, no anger killing, no harsh judgment. The clergy picked up from the myriad understandings of God that portion of divine attributes that worked for them and for their people – the images of a loving, caring, immanent, compassionate God that resided within, between, and amongst those people. We began our prayers with "O Holy One", "O Mystery of Mysteries", "O Nameless One of Many Names", "O God of all Compassion," and we followed with words that described the most encouraging, loving, all-for-you kind of protector God we'd ever known. Big, of course. It was still big. But big in the sense of expansive, not big in the sense of scary. That kind of God was left behind in the neutering booth of feminist theology.

But we'd missed something significant that was happening in those images workshops back in the late 1980s and throughout the ensuing years. We were so busy paying attention to the gender of the deity that we missed the far more significant thing that was being shown us in those pictures people were picking up and describing. When you're not looking for something, chances are you won't see it. We didn't.

What we missed was the fact that those who picked up pictures, who turned to their partners and described their understandings of God, weren't describing a deity, a theistic being, at all. They weren't choosing pictures of strong, regal-looking David Bowie-like androgynous beings sitting on thrones or floating amongst the stars. They weren't pointing to pictures of beings at all. The pictures people picked up and still pick up to share with their partners are much more difficult to describe. They are pictures that depict beauty or love or relationship. They show children laughing or splashing in puddles. They show reflections of light and the mists of the morning. They show aged and crinkling hands clasped by the miniature translucent fingers of a newborn. They show horses against the sunset, and water lapping on shores. They show young men with Down 's syndrome and elderly couples holding hands. They show rocks with stripes and circles and cracks. They show leaves in every

111

different shape and colour imaginable. They show stars against the velvet blackness of the sky. They show moods and feelings and the breathlessness we experience when we feel and acknowledge the presence of God.

And we missed it. Entirely.

It is time we paid attention to what people in our churches showed us when they chose those pictures some twenty-odd years ago and are still showing us now. While they feel and know and experience God, it isn't the God we keep offering them up on Sunday mornings. It isn't the God that rules the world or even the one that set it in motion. It isn't the God that sent them Jesus and it isn't the God who killed him to save them from their sins. It isn't the God that rules the wind and whips together tsunamis and mudslides. It's a feeling, a sense of purpose. It's the welling up of love or the drop-kick of conscience. It's the wonder we experience in the face of all we can never even hope to understand.

One of the peculiarities of that revelation, however, is that those who showed us the pictures very likely could not have articulated the full extent of what they were showing us, either. In 1999, after a particularly difficult and damaging year or two in the life of my presbytery, I, as chair of presbytery, and my colleague, as incoming chair of presbytery, undertook to build some bridges with congregations by taking to them the workshops on core values and core beliefs that came out of the then-Division of Mission in Canada. Over the course of two years we visited all but two of the presbytery's congregations, some individually and some in groups of two or three.

The workshops set before the group a variety of situations and asked them to work them through or respond to them. Situations like this: you overhear a couple of teenagers in a mall talking about how meaningless their lives are and, apparently, agree to commit suicide together. What do you do? Or a small child comes to you at its grandparent's funeral and asks you what happened? You have very little time to respond. What do you say? Values exercises had the groups cull the values they would take with them to a new place over and again until they had refined their list to the last few that were of the greatest import to them.

At the conclusion of the exercise, we had learned much about the values different congregations held, all of which were amazing and strong and focused primarily on loving justly and with compassion. But we had learned far more about the beliefs of those who had been in the pews of those congregations, some of them for decades. And what we learned disturbed us.

Unless someone had been theologically educated or had participated in the work of the church outside of the congregation – in a presbytery, conference, or General Council committee or working unit – their understanding of theology could only be described as elementary. They spoke of a God who lived in heaven, who took those who died to live with him there. Sometimes they spoke of God needing helpers (ostensibly angels) or taking the most beautiful people to be with him. They worried about the final judgment against those who committed suicide. They spoke of God's power to protect, intervene, judge, and discipline. While those same people might have chosen pictures of a being-less God in another workshop, they were only able to present understandings of that God as a being who had agency, the power to act independent of humanity, and who, for the most part, lived somewhere else in the beliefs workshops.

It puzzled us. Both of us had been trained in contemporary understandings of theology. Both of us understood the Bible to be a human, not a divine construction. Both of us contextualized scripture when we read it and offered our interpretations framed by that work. Both of us preached about the activity of God being that which comes about as the result of people choosing to live in right relationship with one another, not as some cosmic intervention in the operation of the world. Both of us had what anyone would very likely describe as non-theistic, non-being, non-interventionist understandings of God. We combined them with rational understandings

113

of Jesus as a very human person rather than as the only begotten Son of God and neither of us had anything near a traditional understanding of salvation or the purposes of the crucifixion. But both of us recognized that somehow we had been complicit in the non-education of the laity.

My colleague, in response, undertook to create an adult Bible study resource that introduces contemporary scholarship, thereby raising awareness of and openness to new understandings of God and the realization that the Bible is a human construction. I turned back to my congregation and sought to identify where, exactly, those elementary theological and Christological ideas were being preserved, if not reinforced, despite my intentionally progressive thinking.

My work was infinitely easier than was my colleague's. It wasn't at all difficult to find those places where the idea of God as a being who intervenes in human affairs, who dwells somewhere other than wherever we are, who created the heavens and the earth, who offered his son as a sacrifice for our sins, etc., etc., was hiding. They were everywhere. That theistic, interventionist God wasn't hiding at all. Indeed, my whole worship service reinforced that kind of a God.

While I had long since dropped the idea of approaching God – after all, where was that god before I started trying to get its attention and what if it was too busy to answer my perfectly crafted invocations, could I have borne the rejection? – no, I didn't offer a prayer of approach – we had simply prepared ourselves to be in God's presence but the prayers I wrote to get us to do that were all about God opening us, calming us, centering us, filling us. There was literally nothing we could do on our own. God did everything and we waited upon God to do it.

Our scripture readings – snippets straight out of the Contemporary English Version and chosen according to the lectionary, were filled with stories of God's anger and wrath, the Flood, the parting of the Red Sea, the challenge on Mount Moriah. They drove home our utter dependence upon a God who might judge or save us, might curse or bless us, might walk with us or deny us entirely. Through the psalmist's voice we were to praise God for an unlimited love and use God as a curse to lay against our enemies. The images and concepts we shared with the congregation during our sermons or our workshops were entirely undermined by what the Good Book demanded we read to them week after week after week. We were, quite simply, losing the battle.

And when we rose to sing! Ah! What challenges befell us then! Our hymns were full of God's interventionist skill, God's creation of the earth, God's grand salvific equation, God's power and strength, and God's illimitable mercy. We could be instruments of that mercy, but we were never its originators. We could see the need for it, but we could never bring it about without the assistance of Our Distant Deity (ODD). Without ODD's hand in our salvation, we were sunk.

What to do? It was clear that almost everything in our liturgy undermined the contemporary understandings of God, Jesus, the Bible, the church that we in congregational ministry were attempting to present. Something had to give.

Unfortunately, what gave was too often the "we in congregational ministry" and, along with us, those for whom those ancient constructs no longer held sway. Over the past couple of decades that latter number has grown incredibly as contemporary scholarship seeped out of hallowed ecclesial halls and began lining up on the shelves of local bookstores. Add the continual publication of an exponential number of web pages dedicated to debunking biblical and religious myths of all kinds and you can see what the issues are. Those who, like clergy, had been exposed to contemporary scholarship were as unwilling as clergy to accept it. Since the majority of what they heard, sang, and read in church mirrored those archaic theological constructs they no longer ascribed to, their numbers in church began to shrink.

115

Clergy though, like my colleague and I, had stayed and many like us had learned to cope with the dissonance between what we were saying and what we believed because really, we still believed what we were saying. For us, there was very little dissonance at all.

Say what? How could we continue to read, sing, and pray in ways that didn't support contemporary understandings? It's simple. We created a code and that code saved us.

Take, for instance, the word "God". When I use that word, I am speaking about that impetus toward good that rises within me and compels me to live in right relationship with myself, with those around me, and with creation. I build that impetus up for myself and for others when I choose to honor the relationship that exists between me and another or an inanimate object. If I honor that relationship, I am strengthening God in the world. If I desecrate it, I am destroying God in the world.

Bet you'd never know that's what I meant when I use that word. At least, like my mother's dining room table, not until I clarified it. When I read the word "God", the cipher in my head does its quick translation and what I'd read was absolutely palatable – it doesn't offend me at all.

When I read biblical stories, I wove the concept of metaphor and myth into my understanding even though, I came to realize, when I preached using metaphor and myth to illustrate my meaning, I rarely, if ever, told the congregation that I believed the original stories to be myth or metaphor. I assumed they knew. They didn't.

Now, I haven't checked with my colleague recently to get his definition of God, but without having done so, I can pretty much say with confidence that he, too, has a cipher at work in his head so that when he reads, sings or says "God" he, too, is comfortably reassured with the quick translation and I know that the metaphor angel has worked her wonders on the biblical stories for him, too. Many of you may have similar ciphers or angels operative inside your own heads. While I'd have no idea what you meant when you said the word God, I would probably guess that it wasn't what I meant. Based on the images workshop, I'd believe that you were talking about an experience or a feeling, a relationship that spoke of life to you. Based on the dog and pony show my colleague and I took through the presbytery, I'd believe you were talking about a supernatural being who intervened in a regular way in the affairs of humans. I simply would not be able to tell you what you meant unless you told me. And it is very likely that due to the lack of conversation between us on issues of such theological import we'd have stalled the opportunity to find out what each other meant long before we would have ever managed to get close to finding out.

That is the crux of the problem. Clergy use the word God in our liturgies and we neglect to say what it is we mean by it. We neglect to point out or allow for the myriad understandings that sit before us on a Sunday morning. We frame the words we use with hymnody written with a completely different image of God in mind than the one we might comfortably adhere to. And we pray and pray and pray as though the words we lift will be heard somewhere and that God in the sky, who we don't really believe in anymore, will answer those prayers at his or her leisure. We do this despite the fact that our understandings of God don't match anything that we are saying or singing or reading aside from, perhaps, our sermons and then we are surprised when people say they don't believe in God anymore. It's no wonder. No wonder at all.

Similarly, we talk endlessly about Jesus but never actually spit out the truth that not only do we not believe he is the divine son of God, we think that he is divisive and problematic in a pluralistic world teetering on the brink of self-destruction as it is. We present him as a human being with some very good things to say to the human condition, but then we wrap our presentation up with hymns like "Giver of the Perfect Gift," which speaks of Jesus as the only hope of humankind; "Hope of the World", which declares that Jesus' cross has saved us; and "God Whose Almighty Word", which calls for the shedding of the light of the gospel wherever it isn't

117

currently known. Our words humiliate our lofty Christologies and theologies and prevent them from being understood at all. They reinforce theistic images of God and salvific images of Jesus, both of which continue to be exclusive and problematic not only for those in leadership in the church, but for those who are finding the pews more and more uncomfortable for all the wrong reasons.

How do we right these challenges in our worship settings? How do we learn to use language that is more inclusive, indeed, radically inclusive, spiritually inclusive, in order that the church can continue to be about the work of speaking to the realities and complexities of human life and engaging people in the task of challenging and changing the world around them in those places it needs to be done? If what we are saying is critically important to human relationship and to all life on the planet, then is it not crucial that we say it in a way that is accessible and easily understood, that will draw people into conversation rather than be so entirely coded as to force people out of conversation? I believe it is.

In order to do that, and there will be many who will not want to, we will have to find language that moves our theistic understanding of God out of its privileged position and replace it with non-theistic language; that is, language that does not look, smell, bark, or wag its tail in a way even remotely like a theistic God. And that, my sisters and brothers, is not going to be easy.

I am not talking about removing God from our stories, our music, our understandings – if you want God there, you will find God there; but it is going to take work because "God" is not going to be so obvious as it once was. God is not going to be handed out on a silver tray like it has been in the past. Because what we have been saying all this time has been so dramatically misunderstood, not only by people in the pews, but by the world around us, that work is now critically urgent regardless of how difficult it is going to be. We have to work at being entirely clear about what we are saying or, better still, make what we are saying broad enough to engage those inside and outside the church who have no need of, or interest in, the theistic God in whom they think we still believe.

How do we do that? The same way we did the gender-inclusive transition.

First, let me tell you what I think church is about. In my understanding of church, which developed in response to my interpretation and reading of the stories about Jesus, church is about transforming lives in order that people can live in radically ethical ways. Living in a radically ethical way means working one's hardest to live out the values they hold sacred or worthy, for which they might, were those values being threatened in a significant way, actually die and stretching one's heart to be big enough to try to ensure that everyone who wants to also has the opportunity to live those values out. It means constantly enlarging one's circle of concern to see yet another person, animal, place, thing, ideal as worthy and work toward honoring and living in right relationship with that worth. That's what I think church is about – challenging people to see that, to live toward it, to hold one another when they fail to do it, and to help them up, over and again, so they can try once more.

The church's responsibility, then, is getting someone into the space where they can learn about, be fed, and work towards living in that radically ethical way, that is, in right relationship with self, others, and the planet. The church's job is to help individuals and communities engage in the spiritual quest of finding where they are most gifted to live in response to the world's greatest need and then, when they've found it, to help them live in that place of connection – not an easy task at all.

But what is REALLY difficult is finding someone's door into that space. Not everyone gets into that spiritual space in the same way. Think of it like music. Not everyone likes the same kind of music. Some are moved to tears by St. Matthew's passion. Others by Leanne Womack's I Hope You Dance. Jazz unleashes some people's soul's, Ska is the key to others. They are all different. It is the same with spirituality – everyone has different doors through which they approach and are nurtured in the spiritual quest. Recognizing this, it is important to note that I am only speaking today about one of the many, many ways that people get into that transformative place. The church is only ONE of the ways that people arrive at the spiritual nexus that is their place of radically ethical living and communal spiritual gatherings (usually called worship) only one of the ways that church can help people do that. That's the one about which I'm speaking.

If we think of our language in worship as offering portals, doors, into that spiritually-rich environment in which people become connected, for many for a long, long time, the biggest door was marked "Big Guy in the Sky". When we began to employ gender-inclusive language, those for whom the concept of a male God was important initially felt lost because those doors were no longer made available to them. They weren't made obvious by clergy, hymns, prayers, readings; they had literally disappeared. In order to get back into that spiritual place, they needed to find new doors. The doors were there, but it took a bit of work to recognize them.

Closing the door marked Male God required people to look for attributes of that Male God through which they could move to continue their spiritual nurture. Those marked, Warrior, Angry King, Fierce Avenger were scarcely ever opened although they might have been. But those marked with attributes that were recognizable as ones a Loving Father God might have offered became the new way to get into the spiritual marketplace. Compassionate One, Holy One, Loving God, Creator of the Universe. We wrote them into our prayers, changed words in our hymns, and moved, not seamlessly, but well, into gender-inclusive communities. When gender-inclusive language is being done well, you don't notice it at all. For that reason, doors marked Mother God never really got the grease they needed to become well-used portals. They simply weren't inclusive. They merely provided an alternative exclusive picture of God.

If we are now going to close up the doors that privilege a theistic God, what do we close and what must we open? It may well be that we don't need to close a lot of doors at all but that we can make a few adjustments and continue to use that same door. Of course, doors marked with those words for which we have had to create code in order to keep them open in the past, like "God", will be closed. And doors that suggest activity of a divine being, like "Creator of the World", "Healer of Our Every Ill", activity we no longer claim to be the direct consequence of God's own hand, will be closed. But doors that are marked with anything that suggests agency, the ability to act as a being, can almost always remain open with very little adjustment and so remain a significant part of our communal spiritual journey. I call them simple shifts. Compassion-ate One becomes Compassion. Holy One become Holiness, Loving God becomes Love.

We find ourselves refining our concept of God by distilling the attributes and behaviors of our theistic God and the challenges it set before us and using them to find our way into the place where we are nurtured, stretched, and moved spiritually. Those things people might call God, they find in other words, phrases, experienc-es in the gathering. Like the shifts with which gender-inclusivity challenged us, these, too, challenge us but, when done well, the absence of theistic language often goes unnoticed. Indeed, as West Hill United Church, the community I serve, moved into the use of spiritually-inclusive language, in several cases, it was only after the media publicized what we were doing that people in the congrega-tion noticed at all. And, when newcomers come into the community, often months or a year after they have been with us, they continue to use the word God in their vocabulary because they hear us talk-ing about God all the time, even though they have not regularly heard the word in our Sunday gatherings. Their understandings of God are reinforced by what we do, but the word itself no longer limits those understandings.

We have also noted that it is often only when someone tells a newcomer to the community that we are not using the word God that they then notice. Sometimes, being told that causes great anxiety. Don't we believe in God? Shouldn't we be talking about God? When engaged in conversation about it, through the exploration of their understandings of God and how they are made present in our services, choices, and behaviors, however, they are easily assured that God is what we are always talking about. They can quickly understand that our choices are made in order to avoid privileging or reinforcing a particular image of God in our services. Because we choose not to privilege those perspectives, individuals who had become weary of constantly translating theistic images and those who have no interest or belief in a theistic God but who wish to be challenged within spiritual community have found a welcoming place in our pews. Many of them, if we were not speaking in the way we speak, would never, ever have considered returning to church.

You have been provided a copy of the language policy that is currently in place at West Hill United Church. The appendices will be available on the More Franchises website and extend the document to over seventy-five pages, which is why they are not reproduced for you here. I will read to you the purpose for and the actual policy itself and leave the rest to you to peruse at your leisure. I was not part of the drafting of this document; indeed, I didn't know it was being written until it was presented to me, in its almost final form, for my input. The process of writing it began when a gender-inclusive issue was raised at a choir practice and the choral director showed immense relief that the congregation had a policy, approved in 1992, that it would use inclusive language in all its official presentations, including music, thereby saving her the need to defend the position. At that time, it was recognized that a policy regarding claims that could not be substantiated, supernatural forces and beings that could not be proven, and theological assumptions that were cast in a pre-Copernican worldview should be in place to assist decision-making and responsiveness in a similarly constructive way. The framework for it was drafted by my partner, Scott Kearns, the congregation's music director, and reviewed, edited, rewritten, amended, added to, and refocused by at least ten theologically and non-theologically trained individuals within the congregation and the Elements of Worship committee before being presented to the Board. Accepted by the Board, it is now the official policy of the church.

*Purpose of the Policy/Guideline*

To equip all those seeking to communicate on behalf of WHUC with guidelines for choosing language that is:

- contemporary and relevant
- accessible to those with or without religious backgrounds
- intellectually and ethically accountable

*Policy*

1. The language we use in all aspects of formal ministry on behalf of West Hill United Church

- will reflect the core values we believe are fundamental to right relationships with self, others, and the world, including justice, compassion, respect, freedom, and community
- will contain no assertion or suggestion that any text
  - o is infallible or inerrant
  - o has inherent authority
  - o is of supernatural origin
  - o that any religious doctrine, tradition, or experience
  - o represents absolute or universal truth
  - o ought to be believed, accepted, sought after, or shared by all
  - o results in guaranteed outcomes if believed or obeyed
- will communicate respect for everyone's right to hold their own viewpoints, beliefs, and interpretations of experience
- will feature relevant and commonly-used vocabulary, with metaphor clearly identifiable as such

2. We welcome the sharing of diverse views and personal beliefs in group discussions and informal settings, with the expectation that all parties involved will demonstrate mutual respect and a desire for learning and growth.

3. We regularly review language used in our formal ministry and make revisions where necessary for greater clarity, relevance, and integrity.

I have gone on record many times saying that I do not really care if the church, as an institution, survives. Indeed, many believe I'm going to singlehandedly destroy it. What I believe needs to survive, and what I am willing to pour my life energy into preserving is the good that the church can do through the transformational work it can bring about in people's lives and in communities because of them. If that work can only survive if we close the door on outdated concepts and words and find new ways to express its urgency, then I am willing to pay that cost. Because I believe the church is perfectly outfitted to do that work, I remain a passionate advocate of it.

The following song by my husband, Scott Kearns, might give you an idea of what that god we always talk really is.

### It is Love

What stands tall when all has fallen,
remains when strength is gone?
What can heal the broken spirit,
'mid chaos find a song?
It is love, and love alone.
It is love, and love alone.

What consoles an aching spirit,
brings joy despite the pain?
What can soothe our hurtfill'd anger,
sees sharing wealth as gain?
It is love, and love alone.
It is love, and love alone.

What inspires responsibility,

124

sees worth in great and small?
What views self and others equally,
seeks peace and joy for all?
It is love, and love alone,
It is love, and love alone.

What will feed our hungry children,
will bind the wounds of war?
What will speak sweet peace in conflict,
what makes the spirit soar?
It is love, respect and care,
within and then with others gladly shared,
at home and ev'rywhere,
It is love, and love alone,
it is love, and love alone,
It is love.[17]

*In the church I would rather speak five intelligible words to instruct others than ten thousand words in a tongue. ...*

---

[17] R. Scott Kearns, *The Wonder of Life* (Toronto: File 14, 2005)

# How Much Baggage
## Does the Spiritual Journey Need?
*North Burlington Baptist Church, 2009*

*(Prior to sharing this content, I had given a brief history of the early years of the CCPC and the factors that had led to its emergence in the Canadian context.)*

... **B**ut the beginning of CCPC and the opening up of this work in Canada was not nearly the beginning of this work for the progressive task has been part of the religious impulse since the first effort was ever made to make sense of the world by a long-distant relative, very likely on the African plain some 200 – 300,000 years ago.

Though I am not an academic theologian, I live and work within a world often defined and bound by theological terms and so my comfort level with them is perhaps higher than that of your typical Burlingtonian. Other than that, I am not a scholar in this area. I read. I enjoy exploring and wondering and uncovering details and piecing together puzzles. But I am not an anthropologist and I need to make that clear. I am a practitioner. I practice ministry, which I am trained and prepared to do. And I pay attention to what is said around me, what my experience is and has been, and how I and others respond to that experience.

Getting back to that distant relative and the world she inhabited, a world we can only imagine. Initially patterning her behavior on instinct, the evolution of reflective thought, the capacity to remember events, to project the possibility of their recurrence into the future, to expect things to happen, would have been a tectonic shift in the way she perceived the world. We who function within normal ranges of psychological, emotional, intellectual, and physical development take these things for granted. It doesn't even cross our minds that we might not remember what happened a few moments ago or that, should we find ourselves approaching a door, we wouldn't know what to do with the shiny round thing sticking out from one side of it. When we no longer know how to operate such things, we know it is the world inside us that has changed. I'm not so sure that our distant relative understood that shift.

So there she stood in a world she was dimly coming to understand and as that understanding grew, so, too, did her desire to prepare herself for what might happen. Her experiences placed before her a multitude of possibilities – a full belly or hunger; shelter or exposure; high ground or floods; water or thirst; poisonous herb or medicinal. Bit-by-bit she cobbled together a vast store of information that could be passed down through the all too brief generations.

But some things she couldn't learn. The whys were always intangible. Why did the rains come some years and not others? Why lightning, or flood, or famine, or dead children? Why poisonous snakes and ravaging beasts? Why roaming bands of marauding warriors? Why pain? Why death? And, in the finality of that last sleep, so many, many more unanswerable questions.

Those questions mark for me the beginning of the spiritual quest. The moment we try to figure out something that our investigative minds can't capture, measure, reproduce with experimental precision, in that moment, we embark upon the spiritual quest. Any of you who have raised children will know how early it begins in a human's life or how early we come to know it begins. As soon as the word "why" becomes part of a child's vocabulary, it becomes one of her or his favorite words. "Why?" "Why?" "Why?" I imagine the quest really begins when the child is still pre-verbal but we, who place such importance on language, tend to mark its beginning by the use of that word.

As primitive beings, the words will most assuredly not have been the same but the impulse would certainly have matched. We want to know why as though our finding out will give us a sense of completion, of resolution. And so, I imagine, that primitive being set about creating answers that settled her mind, brought an ease to her heart.

As with all evolution, branches from the main roots veered off in different directions forming into different traditions. Some of our distant relative's offspring found their comfort in the shelter of the human mind, exploring the depths and recesses of consciousness as a route to a promised fulfillment – the why was to teach us a way toward that fulfillment. Others learned to walk with awe in a world imbued with the holiness of the sacred, each tree, bird, expanse of water filled with a divinity to be honored – the why was to help us to live in harmony with the sacred earth. Some developed complex understandings of deities who were less immanent, living atop mountains or beyond the clouds who would keep the people safe, guarding, cajoling, exacting a price, creating a world our distant relatives could enjoy, but allowing them to live in it at a price – allegiance to the gods and their capricious demands – the why was to please the gods.

Back then, it may have been that we sat smooth stones in a certain pattern around our food cache or hung our flint stones on a certain side of our bodies. It may have been that we burned a particular herb and smudged the ashes on the tops of our feet and along the insides of our arms. It may have been that we captured and released our first fish of the run or sacrificed it on a polished altar. It may have been that we stood naked under the forest's oldest tree through the year's longest night. Whatever the journey required, we carried it in our pack – it became part of our spiritual baggage, necessary for our survival.

One of the key elements for survival was the concept of communal worship. Despite the fact that the word worship likely didn't come into use until about the year 1200 CE, the ritual act of gathering a community together to reinforce what behavior was required to appease the gods and keep the people safe had likely been happening since before recorded time.

The word actually tells us what the action was all about. Its root is from the Saxon word *weord(th)*, or worthy – to be equal in value to, with *scipe* adding the sense of being in the condition of being equal in value to. So through worship we come to be in the condition of being equal in value to or offer something that is in the condition of being equal in value to.

To what? That seems obvious – the gods, or, in our particular case, a single deity known as God.

But what could possibly be of equal value to god or worthy of being offered to balance what god has given. If we do a quick check over the things we have (remember, we're back about five thousand years here) we attribute our families, our community, our livelihood, our crops, our animals, our wealth, our health, our world, our sunshine, our rain - you're getting this, right? Absolutely everything in our life can be attributed to god, so whatever we offer has to be pretty big in order to balance what it is god has given us.

And the only thing that can possibly balance that is the whole of not only your life, but the life of the community and, beyond that, the lives of the world, through you. The covenantal agreement.

So worship, long before it ever got that name, was about gathering the people together to remind them of the importance of that piece of work. If god was to continue to care for them, to offer them the things they needed to live, if they were to continue to have the gifts they had, then they were going to need to act in these particular ways, eat these particular things, not touch these other particular things, behave in these particular ways on these particular days, observe these particular feasts, wear these particular clothes when doing these particular things, and be very, very particular about it all.

The task was of utter importance for the fate of both the community and every individual in it rested upon it. For many, to this very day, it remains so. Indeed, at some point, the stakes grew exponentially as the costs associated with failure to attend to these duties during one's lifetime were understood to be associated with the account coming due upon one's death. This still remains a potent piece of religious baggage.

What once, long before anyone would have ever named it the starting point of a spiritual journey, may have been merely a flight of imagination set off by the simple consideration of the meaning of things, became a grueling task to which humanity, in so many different ways, has set its shoulders for millennia.

Now, it is obvious that we no longer carry around everything in our pack that we once did; nor do the other religious traditions that branched off from our distant spiritual relative so long ago. Religions evolve. Their understandings of the world challenge them to. We can see it in our own spiritual documents and our responses to them. The biblical text, in its admonitions, very likely sets up prohibitions against behavior previously understood to be requirements if not acceptable practices within the religious cult. The sacrifice of Isaac is likely the most obvious one and a prohibition against what may have been a regular religious practice at the time – child sacrifice.

There are other things set out in the biblical record that we have taken out of our packs and no longer practice because we have deemed them no longer appropriate for ourselves, using our own moral compass to discern what is right and what is wrong. A mere 25 verses after the 10 commandments, Exodus 21:17 tells us that any child who curses his mother or father shall be put to death. While we may feel very much like doing so from time to time, we have pretty much stepped away from the biblical imperative on that one. Our baggage has been lessened as we have considered, reflected, found ideas wanting and made our own choices. We have realized much of the error in our religious heritage: Exodus 21 also giving us much to consider in regard to our slaves and the children we sell into slavery; other sections reminding us of the place of women; the sin of the spilling of "seed" (also known as male masturbation or any form of birth control other than abstinence); the naming of homosexuality as an abomination; the condemnation of those who have divorced; and the obligatory remarriage of the widowed to the deceased's brother. These practices we have found to be irresponsible or immoral and we, those of us who have considered them carefully beyond the assumption of the infallibility of the bible, have denounced them. The bible is not our moral compass, has not been for centuries and definitely should not be.

But I digress. Back to our spiritual baggage.

Just what do we need to keep in that spiritual pack of ours in order to move forward on the spiritual journey? What is it that we need?

We began with the word "why". The answer, our answer within our tradition, was to please the gods. So our baggage helped us with that answer — we had tools and practices, ways of worshipping and caring for the world that helped us do that, helped us make our god happy, pleased him and, more recently, her. Literature, websites, worship services, whole ministries are devoted to helping us learn how to please god with our lives, the whole of our lives, in the same way that our distant relative and the rest of her community sought to do so long ago. And, in the course of our work, we have created some exquisitely beautiful, intricate, amazingly wonderful ways in which to do that.

Music of adoration flowed from the bows, keyboards, and lips of some of humanity's most gifted composers and performers. Painters illuminated scenes with utmost reverence and sculptors eased passion from the depths of utterly cold marble. Compassion welled up in the hearts of our most beloved laborers who, in their tiny corners, made the world a more peaceful place. Inspired by the

131

gifts they found in their spiritual backpacks, they left behind trails of beauty we yet enjoy and revere.

They were pleasing their god. They were living out their covenant with that god. They were following the Jesus they found in the scripture, one of the many portrayals found there.

But I am concerned. Deeply concerned for our spiritual journeys today. Much that remains in them is still focused on the task of placating, of appealing to, god and we, those of us trained in liberal seminaries, those of us who have read ourselves beyond the boundaries of traditional Christian literature, those of us who have poked at the corners, pushed the envelope, peeked in the closet, whatever metaphor you might like to use, we know there is something amiss and that it must be addressed. Now. Because if we don't do something about it now, we will merely become bent and bowed by a worthless baggage, affecting our own private worlds, but having little effect on the world at large. If that is your aim, fine, carry on. If that is not your aim, then hear me out.

Our answer to the "why" question has changed. When we look at the bible and we examine its sources and we come up with the very credible response that it is not the authoritative word of god for all time, much less for all people; when we determine that only it ever proves its god's existence; when we examine it ever so carefully and measure what it says against our principles and find that there is much more of it that is wanting, that sets up destructive, tribal, divisive power and violence-based relationships; when we find ourselves rejecting most of what it says because, unless we come up with a pretty elaborate metaphorical interpretation of the story we're reading, we have a viscerally negative response to it, we have to ask ourselves what we're doing, trying to please that kind of a god. In fact, when we really press, we find the whole concept of god to be a human construct, a very good one, created for a very good reason at a time when it was needed, but one that, now, in this time and in a shrinking world with even more rapidly shrinking resources, is more than unhelpful – is actually, in many respects, destructive. Without that god, pleasing that god can no longer be the answer to that primal question, "Why?", for our old answer no longer works. And as it fades in merit, we must question, too, the tools and burdens we have carried thus far on our spiritual journeys.

In reality, I am not certain there is an answer to that why? question. Or at least not an answer that will satisfy everyone equally. Many will want to remain safely ensconced in a world protected by a divine being who they believe is committed to their care both now and in a life to come beyond this one. Many others will expect to return to this world over and again, working through fulfilling the many steps toward achieving their ultimate fulfillment, the why to which they have been heading over the millennia.

But what of us? We who have explored the world for the most part, under the banner of a god whose existence we now question if we don't outright deny. What is our why? What will set out our reasons for living?

Perhaps if we go back to the definition of the word 'worthy' we can renegotiate the connection for which we seek. If you recall, we were discerning what would be worthy of offering that might equal what god offered us in our lives. Since we believed we were dependent upon god for everything, we could offer nothing short of our lives. If, now, we remove god from the equation, leaving the whole of our lives there on the scale for the moment, what, if anything could be set in the place of that deity that might be worthy of the whole of our lives? What would be equal in value to our lives? For what would we spill out our life energy? Is this not, in fact, the primal story of our faith tradition, the pouring out of a single man's life energy in the pursuit of what he believed to be worthy of his life – a vision of a world he sought to bring about? Now it is our turn. What is it that we would place on the other side of the equation that is worthy of our lives? Why DO we live? WHY?

I believe we live to bring about a more beautiful world. I believe we live to build love into the world. I believe we live to create right relationships with one another, with ourselves and with the world. I believe that to do these things, the tools we need in our pack are few. We don't need particular hymns or prayers or even hymns at all. I don't think we need particular ways of being in community but I do think we need the radical truth that community can offer us as it exposes us to who we really are and challenges us to speak openly and honestly with one another. And so these two things I place in my pack – love and community. And you, whoever you are, get to figure out how you want to pad those or keep them simple, but those two things are all I believe we really need.

Some days
it seems we have been gently urged into being,
invited to savour the delicacy of life.
Other days
it seems we are flung, flailing, into the fray of life,
its realities searing us with truth.
Wisdom's beauty mars our virgin souls,
patterns woven as the rich, soft lustre of innocence
gives way to each crevasse of knowing.
Innocence.
Experience.
Merged, they mould us into who we are,
determine how we touch the world's waiting face
and what the quality of life we will bring forth.
May we greet each day as gift and blessing,
fold its promise into who we will become,
and live the fullness of its teachings
that our touch
might bring beauty,
and our prayer,
a song.[18]

---

[18] Gretta Vosper, *Another Breath* (Toronto: File 14, 2009)

# Fraying Claims to Truth:

## Challenging Progressives Beyond Their Chosen Response
## to the Burning of the Koran

*Published in 2010 on the website of The Center for Progressive Christianity.*
*Reprinted with permission.*

It was a few days before September 11th that I began writing an article addressing the issues raised by the threatened burning of Korans in Florida. I had hoped, at that time, that nothing would have come of it, that Pastor Terry Jones would have decided against going ahead with his plan to "honor" the 9/11 victims of the World Trade Centre terrorist attack with his congregation by putting the sacred writings of Islam's prophet, Mohammed, to the torch. The day has now passed. The fire was not lit, but one Arab professor has been killed in an altercation regarding the controversy as the world, again, is pulled into the destructive vortices of vitriolic religious debate.

As the Florida congregation prepared to gather tinder for their incendiary gesture, religious and spiritual progressives, like the Network of Spiritual Progressives of which I am a member, decided upon their own gesture – agreeing to gather together to read from one another's holy books. The action was intended to symbolically hold up what it is the three Abrahamic faiths have in common, to bring respect and tolerance to the fore, and to expose Pastor Jones' threats as the intolerant rant of a dangerous fundamentalist religious mindset, something most, I think, already know.

But let's take a look at some of what *could* have been read at the Saturday gatherings of such interfaith heroes as Michael Lerner of the Network of Spiritual Progressives. No doubt the texts were very carefully chosen and these would *not* have made the cut. If they had been, people gathered to hear what Islam, Judaism, and Christianity have in common might have found themselves somewhat shocked.

From the Torah:

*When the Lord your God brings you into the land you are entering to possess and drives out before you many nations ... and when the Lord your God has delivered them over to you and you have defeated them, then you must destroy them totally. Make no treaty with them, and show them no mercy... This is what you are to do to them: Break down their altars, smash their sacred stones, cut down their Asherah poles and burn their idols in the fire. (Deuteronomy 7:1-5)*

From the Bible:

*But when John saw many of the Pharisees and Sadducees coming to where he was baptizing, he said to them: "You brood of vipers! Who warned you to flee from the coming wrath? Produce fruit in keeping with repentance. And do not think you can say to yourselves, 'We have Abraham as our father.' I tell you that out of these stones God can raise up children for Abraham. The ax is already at the root of the trees, and every tree that does not produce good fruit will be cut down and thrown into the fire. (Matthew 3:7-10)*

From the Koran:

*I will cast terror into the hearts of those who disbelieve. Therefore strike off their heads and strike off every fingertip of them. This is because they acted adversely to Allah and His Messenger; and whoever acts adversely to Allah and His Messenger-- then surely Allah is severe in requiting (evil). This-- taste it, and (know) that for the unbelievers is the torment of the fire. (Sura 8.0012-8.0014)*

It is clear from these readings, and dozens more like them, that the little church in Florida wasn't that far off the mark. Neither would a mosque be off the mark if they chose to burn the Torah, Judaism's sacred scripts. And if a synagogue got a brazier going for the purposes of torching the Gospel, well, their choice to do so would be well within the commands attributed to the God to whom members of all three faiths bow in adoration.

The truth of the matter is that the scriptures of Judaism, Christianity, and Islam are filled with violence, divisiveness, condemnation. So, too, are they filled with passages that condone the destruction of property and persons of other belief systems and nationalities. True, too, is the reality that such content can, as Jones has reminded us, be used for appalling purposes. The good pastor was only doing what he believed his God expected him to do. And if we think that we were persuasive in getting him to call his plan to a halt, we need to think again. Jones wouldn't deny his God for anyone. Not for his president, Barak Obama, who pleaded with him on behalf of Americans around the world, not to go ahead with his plan. Not for his evangelical brother in the faith, Rick Warren, who called it a "cowardly act". Not for any "progressive" Christian like me or Diana Butler Bass who drives a car with a COEXIST bumper sticker on it, each of the letters formed from the symbol of a different religion. And he would certainly not deny his God for a progressive Jew like Michael Lerner who is bringing together Jews and Muslims and Christians to participate in what Jones could only ever think was against God's plan. The plan was not cancelled because of any arguments against it. Indeed, it was not cancelled at all. It was simply changed and only because Jones felt "God was telling [him] to stop". God's plan is God's plan as far as Jones is concerned and Jones won't deny his God. Even if it means changing your mind on network news. The frightening reality *we* must acknowledge and face is that he has come to know that capricious God through the Bible, a text most Christians would argue has the right to be called sacred.

Perhaps there was something to the argument that scripture should not be translated into the vernacular. William Tyndale was burned at the stake in 1536 because he translated significant chunks of the Bible into English. He did it so the Bible could be placed it in the hands of common folk, a place we have long understood it belonged. But I'm beginning to wonder if Tyndale was wrong after all. Not that I'd have had him burned for it, of course, but if he'd known the price of placing a Bible in *any*one's hands, including the hands of those who would use it to fan the flames of hatred, maybe he'd have thought twice about it.

Perhaps Tyndale was the first Christian Pandora who, with the best of intentions, opened a box of misery that plagues us yet. Maybe the texts that are too obviously claimed to be the authoritative word of God for all time (TAWOGFAT), or of Mohammed, or Bahá'u'lláh, or Joseph Smith, or whomever, should only be accessible by those who are not going to take them literally, who have been educated beyond the illusions that such books contain revelatory material out of which we can mine morality or privilege. Perhaps they should only be read by those who are disabused of the notion that there is any sort of being that rules the universe and spends his (or her) days dividing us up into those who are right and those who are wrong. Perhaps if the books of all religions were translated only into Latin or some other now-dead language that was understood only by a cloistered, educated elite, the world would be a safer place. After all, ignorance, with a few verses of holy writ in its fisted hand, is not bliss; it's danger.

Of course, we cannot go back. We can't use the memory deleting techniques of science fiction to suck scripture out of the brains of anyone not schooled in the use of the tools of critical scholarship. We're stuck with totally accessible holy scriptures. For better or worse, the words attributed to God or to God's prophets are with us to stay.

But we *can* take away the power of those words, defuse them, expose them for what they truly are. It is a job we must do – those of us who care even a fig about the future and who understand a little bit about these texts. It is not something that is going to be easy and it's not something that is going to happen overnight, but happen it must. The alternative is the use of "holy" texts – ours, yours, theirs, whoever's – as weapons of mass destruction and as missiles of hatred and oppression.

I can swing the word "god" around with the best of them. It doesn't frighten me. And when I read descriptions of God by those who have studied and grappled with the complexity of the concept, I can almost, not quite, but almost, nod in agreement. If someone argues that "god" refers to what is coming into being through the evolution and exquisite nature of life on the planet, I'm good with that. If someone argues that "god" is the good we do in the world, I can accept that too. It's only when the author, Jewish or Muslim or Christian, turns the argument slightly and starts speaking about that big "G" God's *desire* for us to do something, be something, understand something, that I begin to squirm with discomfort. I don't accept the premise that a *concept* has will, or agency, or the power to act. My understanding of god, if I am going to use that word at all, is the good that I can call out of my life, build through my actions, create within my context, bless into being with the whole of who I am. It isn't a remote being who wills me to be a certain way, good though that idea may be. Most well-educated liberal theologians – Jewish, Christian, Muslim – don't believe that's what god is, either, but they continue to capitalize the word and to ground their arguments in texts they still name "holy", "sacred", "scripture", "authoritative".

And there's the rub. We don't get to have it both ways. Either the Torah, the Bible, the Koran, and any other books identified as divinely ordained are just that or they aren't. If they aren't the authoritative word of some divine being or divinely-inspired prophet, then we who are the heirs of the critical scholarship that has taken us to new understandings need to stop acting as though they are. Every time we ground an argument in these ancient texts, every time we come up with a new definition for "god" that doesn't support a literal reading of the texts, every time we process a Bible into a worship space, reverence a mezuzah, speak of the Koran as having been "revealed", we are reinforcing the authority anyone can then claim, which then gives those documents a power they do not deserve. In fact, we are arguing that anyone has the right to do so. After all, the fundamentalists are the ones doing what the text says. We who speak of our texts as metaphor and myth are the ones who have to work to make something else out of what is written.

The needs of our world demand more from us. They demand more than our gathering together and reinforcing the authority of these ancient texts by reading bits and pieces chosen from them that speak of love and compassion, justice and acceptance while covering up the destructive undertones in the rest of those same texts. They demand that we gather together *as people of good faith*, in the largest most secular sense of that phrase, to talk about and explore exactly what those needs of the world are, and then try to find ways to address them.

It won't be a particular religion or creed or nationality or race or ability or sexuality or gender that will forge a sustainable future for life on this planet. We all must work on that together. That the "authoritative" texts of religion can still, in the twenty-first century, deny rights to anyone on the basis of those many things – religion, creed, nationality, etc. – is proof that those texts cannot be used as sources for our direction. The only thing we have that will help us find our way is a deep and reverent sense of love for one another and the desire to honor and protect one another's dignity and rights. And if there is anything in our ancient texts that supports that work, let's read it right alongside all the wonderful, rich, inspirational poetry and prose that has ever been written as we, humanity, have sought to express our appreciation for the deep sacred beauty that is life.

# Promise? What promise?

*Progressions, 2012*

This is the beginning of Advent, the season during which Christians "prepare the way" for Jesus to come. For some, this references the original birth of Jesus, offering an opportunity to celebrate that he came into the world to save it; for others, it refers to the second coming of Jesus, purported to be happening at God's appointed time. And then, of course, there are those who have never given it much thought but who still light the candles and open the little advent windows on their calendars every year. Perhaps it's the chocolate...

A post-theistic Christian understanding will need to let go of the idea that Jesus came at all at the behest of a divine being or that there is a Kingdom of God which he is going to usher in, not during the life he led on earth or in the second coming that has been biblically promised. Indeed, a post-theist perspective, while it may acknowledge Jesus' life, will disallow any supernatural qualities his life has been purported to have.

The idea of preparing for his coming – whether re-enacting the first time or waiting for the second – simply makes no sense once the idea of a supernatural being dissipates. There is no promise made and so no need to keep it. This isn't a huge leap for those steeped in the liberal Christian tradition which has, for many decades, explored Jesus as a visionary and revolutionary killed for his blast-the-status-quo teachings.

Still, many clergy who may at other times of the year describe themselves as post- or non-theists tend to get all wishy-washy about their progressive ideas around Christmas and choose to present the biblical narratives as a single string of events that is as close to being literally true as they can muster. The fear it would seem, is that parishioners, particularly those who come at no other time of the year, want the myths to be carefully dusted off and presented as they always have been with bath-robed shepherds and angelic-for-the-moment angels. It's a real fear and I know it personally. I've also lived past the ire of those who didn't get what they wanted at 11:00 on Christmas Eve, starry, starry skies notwithstanding and yes, it can be done.

The truth is, we all yearn for the security and strength promised in the Christmas readings and the fact that we do exposes the reason that such passages were written – to offer confidence to people who had no earthly reason to be confident. It is obvious even in this much-loved text that God has not made good on the promises with which he has entranced his people. But if the people will just hold out a little longer, he promises, again, that he will send the justice and righteousness he's so far held out on. One could wonder just how long the people were willing to wait.

The answer is – they're still waiting and it's been a long, long time.

Too often, when in a situation of oppression or abuse, the individual or group being oppressed, if they are offered a promise of support or goodwill, will hold onto that promise through thick and thin. Consider the cycle of relationship abuse. The abuser beats up the victim, follows this with remorse, and then promises never to do it again. The victim withstands the abuse, listens to the remorse, often feels guilty for whatever it was the abuser says sparked the violence to begin with, and quickly embraces the abuser again. It can go on for years. (Doesn't it freak you out how neatly the pattern fits the story of God and his people? And how embarrassing it is when you realize how long it took you to see it? Me, too.)

But the person writing the passage may have been truly trying to create a sense of hope within a community rather than reinforcing a theological construct that no longer matters. If you're preaching it the way it's usually preached, you're guilty of the latter, not the former. Like so many other passages in the lectionary, this one needs some significant truth-telling. Read the exegetical material. Learn who wrote it, when, and why, and share with your congregation what you feel is important from that exploration. When you're finished doing that, have the real conversation with them.

Where can we look for such confidence now? Having given up the idea of an omnipotent, omniscient, omni-everything divine being, we have to give up the promise, too. And we don't yet have anything to replace it with.

God, in the past, was the source of goodness, the agent that was going to provide it, promising that, eventually, everything would work out in your favor, if you just believed. In a post-theistic perspective, we see that *we* are now the source of goodness and evil in the world, nothing is identified as one or the other thing without our saying it is so, which leaves us the creators of both good and evil. And we, in a post-theistic world, have the responsibility for bringing good about – creating it out of nothing, standing in the face of evil and denouncing it. We have the responsibility for bringing goodness to those who need it and protecting them from those things that would deny them life or beauty or truth. The problem is, however, that that's as far as we can go in replacing that divine being we spun out of nothing. We cannot promise, as that previous paradigm did, that everything will be okay no matter how hard we work at it; we can't rely on everyone else to be as good as we might hope we can be and even if we could, we still won't be able to take away suffering or create meaning for it where there is none. All we are is potential. Potential, and nothing more.

So, as Advent unfolds, you're going to have to come to grips with the fact that, carols or no carols, shepherds or no shepherds, we're all the answer we've got and we now know it. History has graphically shown us, more than we'd like to admit, that we can't always be relied upon when the cards are down. And the cards are down. At least most rational, science-confirmed cards indicate that our world is challenged by global warming, resource depletion, and a peaking population. It's not going to be pretty. So where do we turn for comfort in such a time?

I believe we are called to be honest with one another. Change is coming and at a cataclysmic rate. Since that's the case, what do we have to lose? Security in a desperate world will be tenuous at best. With that as the situation before us, let's choose to be reckless now, risk the comforts we once had, stand up to the corporate powers that keep us on the track to ruin. It's in us. I know it is.

I often wonder what the world would be like if we had never invented an otherworldly promise of "everything's gonna be alright". If only we had ever been able to cooperate in achieving what we otherwise couldn't alone, facing disease, starvation, and danger, with only those around us and no imagined supernatural being who would save us. Perhaps then we would never have risked the beauty of what we had, what we experienced, what we knew, for a dream of something else. Perhaps we would never have felt the loss of that security nor reached, in repeated destructive successions, for things we thought might make us feel safe again. Maybe we wouldn't have learned to live care-less-ly as though there was another planet – or another life – waiting.

# The Perfect Storm

*I presented this and the following speech, A Noble Truth, at the conference of the Canadian Centre for Progressive Christianity in Halifax, August, 2013.*

Come up with three negative factors that are about to happen all at the same time and you've got what is known as a perfect storm. Moments before the service is about to begin, you realize the PowerPoint isn't yet loaded into the hall computer, the network is down, the computer geek is at his cottage. Three things. Alone, not one of them would be a problem – you'd download the PowerPoint from the network, install it on the computer and be off. Or, even with two things down – the PPT and the network, you'd tap the computer fairy on the shoulder and he or she would have the network up and running in no time. All three and it's a sudden disaster.

A perfect storm is defined as the convergence of a set of negative variables that, alone, may have little or no effect but that together create enormous impact. Although the phrase has been in use for almost three hundred years it became a household term following the publication of Sebastian Junger's book, *The Perfect Storm*, in 1997. Junger brought to life the story of the 1991 Hallowe'en Nor'Easter, a storm that hit the east coast of North America, sinking the ship the Andrea Gail, and taking the lives of all on board.

145

What made the Hallowe'en Nor'Easter the definitive perfect storm were the three separate elements that whipped it into a frenzy:

- warm air from a low-pressure system coming from one direction,
- a flow of cool and dry air generated by a high-pressure from another direction, and
- tropical moisture provided by Hurricane Grace

Each, on its own, would not have created the kind of devastation that the Hallowe'en Nor'Easter wreaked. Together, they were deadly.

More and more frequently, we are watching several weather systems come together to create perfect storm conditions – think Sandy which, alone, was not responsible for everything that happened in the fall of 2012. Hurricane Sandy, coming up from the Caribbean, was met with an unusually early winter storm arriving from the west and an incredibly strong Arctic air force descending upon the same region from the North. One, two, three, catastrophe.[19]

A few years ago (2007), of the 2000 or so words and phrases submitted to Michigan's Lake Superior State University, nineteen affronts to the English language were identified in its annual jab at media, sports, advertising, and politics. At the top of the list was the phrase "perfect storm".[20]

It's not hard to see why the phrase "perfect storm", ten years later, earned itself the notoriety of the Lake Superior State University's (LLSU) award. It was 2007 and sub-prime mortgages

---

[19] Bryan Walsh, "Frankenstorm: Why Hurricane Sandy Could Be the Perfect Storm, Part II, *Time,* October 26, 2012. http://science.time.com/2012/10/26/frankenstorm-why-sandy-could-be-the-perfect-storm-part-ii/#ixzz2btErp71r. Accessed August 13, 2013

[20] Andrew Stern, "Wordsmiths, avoid these words ..." Reuters, Chicago, January 10, 2008. http://www.reuters.com/article/2008/01/01/us-list-idUSN0160393320080101 accessed, Aug 13, 2013

had begun to default, bringing into question the triple-A ratings they had been given that allowed banks to reduce their capital cushions and risk more money. That, and several other factors, made the phrase perfect for use. Even now, five years after LLSU pleaded with journalists to stop using it, web blogs and newspaper articles are still full of it with the trio of Energy, Finance, and the End of Growth being touted as the biggest perfect storm yet.

Maybe, but I think we here can finger off three significant issues in three significant areas that, combined, will create a perfect storm like humanity has never yet seen so I'm boldly going to go where LLSU has begged us not to go. So I'm going to define another Perfect Storm.

Put your fingers in the air, you're going to help me out here. Perfect Storm number 1 – *The Planet* – put up your other hand:

- o   Finger 1 on the second hand – global population;
- o   Finger two on that same hand – resource depletion;
- o   Finger three, again, same hand – resource destruction:

That's Perfect Storm number 1: put your second hand down.

Back to your first hand. That first finger is still up, right? Perfect Storm number 2 – *Society* – Put up finger 2 on that first hand and put up your second hand again:

- o   Finger 1 – global communications networks;
- o   Finger 2 – disintegrating personal support networks;
- o   Finger 3 – a leadership deficit

That's Perfect Storm number 2: put the fingers on your second hand down again.

Back to your first hand. Those two fingers are still up. Perfect Storm number 3 – here it is – *Religion* – Put up finger 3 on that hand and raise your second hand again:

- o   Finger 1 – relevance depletion;

147

o   Finger 2 – loss of community hub capabilities;

o   Finger 3 – theological, liturgical, and spiritual masturbation.

Rest your hands.

If you thought Sandy was bad, the vortex we are potentially heading into now is Sandy to the *n*th degree but it's not just weather, this time. It's happening in the arena of human civilization.

## The Planet

So, the perfect storm and the planet. Many of you will be familiar with the stories and statistics surrounding climate change and global warming. Just this week, Obama tweeted:

Gravity exists. The Earth is round. Climate change is happening. I don't need to convince most of you of that reality. But there are a few things that might make the idea of a perfect storm in relation to the planet a little more graphic and you may or may not know these things. If you're familiar with them all, consider this an opportunity to thread them all together on one string. Or should I say noose.

## Global population

We reached a population of 7 billion people on the planet on Hallowe'en 2011. Between 1959 and 1999, the population of the world doubled. We're not growing at the same rate now, though, so it's expected it will take another 43 years to increase the population by another 50% of what it is now. Eight billion is expected to be reached by 2024. The highest populations are China, India, and the United States of America. By 2030, India's population is expected to surpass China's and by 2050, Nigeria, with its 6% fertility rate is expected to surpass the USA with its fertility rate below 2%. Canada has a low fertility rate at 1.66% which is why immigration is so important to us.[21]

Population control is considered one way to implement care for the planet and its resources. We'll come back to that later.

---

[21] Worldometers. http://www.worldometers.info/world-population/ Accessed August 13, 2013

Everything we consume is somehow related to the earth, whether from the deposits left within it ages and ages ago by previous epochs of life to the renewable resources we cultivate on its surface on a day-to-day basis. There are two things that we need to have in order to use our resources in a stable and balanced way – a tap and a sink. Not a water tap and a drain pipe, though the image helps. The tap is the source or the resource. The sink is where the effluent or the garbage created by production ends up.

Thus the environmental *limits* to economic growth manifest themselves as either: (1) shortages in the "sources" or "taps" of raw materials/natural resources, and thus a problem of depletion, or (2) as a lack of sufficient "sinks," to absorb wastes from industrial pollution, which "overflow" and cause harm to the environment.[22]

Resource depletion is the concern that we are running out of resources.

Rather than give you an exhaustive and exhausting list of areas where shortages are going to begin or have already begun showing up, I'll note a few examples with which you may not be familiar but which add to the element of resource depletion as a facet of the perfect storm. Oil – many believe we are already past peak oil and the use of shale fracturing methods and the mining of dirty oils like the Tar Sands are an indication that the quest for stocks that are more difficult to attain is on. Water. Much of the freshwater used in some areas of the world is tapped from ancient aquifers that contain water that fell thousands of years ago. Saudi Arabia used its aquifers to develop itself as an independent agricultural state. By the 1990s, 75% of its water was mined from prehistoric sites. By 2008, almost all that water was gone and Saudi Arabia was forced to go back to purchasing much of its wheat.

---

[22] Fred Magdoff, "Global Resource Depletion: Is Population the Problem?" *Monthly Review*, Volume 64, Issue 08, January, 2013. http://monthlyreview.org/2013/01/01/global-resource-depletion Accessed August 13, 2013

Countries, like Saudi Arabia and Egypt, which have a per capita arable land of less than half an acre, now purchase land leases from poor countries. Remember the strangeness of the stories of Joseph whose brothers came to him in Egypt to purchase grain during a time of famine. His brothers would now purchase a land lease that might, when exercised, prevent local peasants from growing their own food or managing their own water resources.

And then, there's phosphate. It is expected to be mined out by the end of the century. Anyone know what phosphate is required for? Fertilizer. Without phosphate, we don't grow anything. At least not on depleted land that is only fertile with the addition of massive quantities of phosphate. And that's a lot of land.

## Resource Destruction

Here we look at effluent – the dirt left behind when you create something. Even Michelangelo left some dust lying around when he chipped David out of a solid piece of marble. Creativity produces refuse, dirt, and debris and we need to find ways to deal with that debris.

For millennia, middens lay just outside the habitable area of a village or even, perhaps, in the back yards of homes and estates. What was consumed by the inhabitants ended up in a pile not far enough away from where they slept to allow for carelessness in considering what would be dumped there. Middens now help us read what former populations ate, how they lived, what sustained them. Archaeologists are the most respectable dumpster divers among us.

But something happened along the way. We can't keep our middens far enough away to live healthy lives anymore. We now breathe our detritus, literally. The amount of carbon dioxide in our air has increased by twenty-five percent since 1960. Food sources are often contaminated with chemicals that bleed, unabsorbed, from the earth or that are concentrated in "food chain" sinks. Illness, maturation rates, global warming, and cancers are evidence of our inability to adequately attend to the massive quantities of debris – massive or microscopic – we create.

These three things create a perfect storm in terms of our planet.

On its own, the growth in world population would not be an issue as long as we could continue to grow and develop food sources and materials needed by the growing demands.

On its own, resource depletion could be managed if we developed alternative renewable sources to meet some or all of the needs currently fulfilled by non-renewable or ancient sources.

On its own, resource destruction, while a dreadfully difficult problem to deal with, could be addressed if consumption habits were reduced to a manageable level and here's where we get back to Global population...

Ninety percent of the world's population consumes only 40% of the world's resources. Forty percent of what we currently consume wouldn't be a problem. It's the other ten percent of the population – the top ten in terms of wealth – about 700 million people – that is the biggest problem. They consume a full 60% of our resources and so contribute 60% of the effluent or pollution. The more money you have, the more you consume. It's not a straight-line graph but it's pretty close. It is this group – and most of you are in it – whose consumption patterns most dangerously threaten the planet's resources and contribute to threateningly high $CO_2$ levels in the atmosphere. If we were able to hold those 700 million people to the level of consumption of the other 6 and a half billion people on the planet who knows what might be possible. The perfect storm would most certainly be averted.

Any one or two of these and we're okay. All three and it is catastrophe.

*Society*

*Global communication networks*

At first blush, the development over the past ten years of global communications systems seems like only a win-win for societies everywhere. From the villagers in remote communities in Africa who can now get malaria testing on a cell phone to the explosion of global political activism, the benefits are fairly easy to see. In his book *The Third Industrial Revolution*, social thinker Jeremy Rifkin explores the incredible successes and benefits to the world of a global communications network where the information you have can be had by anyone anywhere almost simultaneously. It is a revolution in information sharing that can and has altered political, social, and personal landscapes.

Over the past few years, however, the loss of personal security and privacy has ballooned not only out of proportion to anything we have ever seen before but also out of control. Teach someone some specific computing skills and they can get pretty much any information about anyone they want. Those who may be brazen in the face of identity theft, confident no one would want their social insurance number or pathetic pension benefits, might feel a bit more concern if a regime change made it illegal to congregate for the purposes of spreading ideology the regime finds distasteful; might feel less secure if their private Facebook posts or emails were being screened for content considered seditious by a government no longer for the people, by the people (I know, that's an American thing but it's good). Indeed, prior to the 2010 G20 in Toronto, individuals whose only activities were congregating to share ideas about how to change some of the prejudicial givens in society, were arrested, detained and, some of them, sentenced to jail time following plea bargains that allowed others of them to go free. Sharing ideas became illegal in the days leading up to that disastrous June weekend. Many of us are in the business of sharing ideas. Some of us might participate in activities considered illegal – like remaining in a park past midnight – in order to bring the serious nature of their ideas to the attention of others. Edward Snowden has helped us see how pervasive the global monitoring system is and how the biggie web-based companies like Google, and Microsoft, are part of the issue. In the States a couple of months ago, a judge ordered Yahoo, Microsoft, and Google to disclose records so that a company found guilty of environmental destruction could, in turn, sue the individuals who built the case against them. Did you forward a petition to raise awareness of the unethical behavior of mining companies in Central America? Are you at risk?

One of the most insidious of the problems with global media is hidden in your search engine and you likely aren't even aware. Back in the day, when web pages were young and we were eagerly lapping up all that access to new information, web creators embedded specific words into the code of the site so that search engines would bring them up. It was a rush to see a site you were involved with show up at the top of a Google search. It meant that, of all the web pages out there, yours was the one Google found to be the most important, most relevant, most visited site ON THE NET! That was pretty extreme.

But over the years, Google, and Yahoo, and Bing, and, yes, even the diplomatic Jeeves, have learned how to give you that exciting rush every time you search for something. You get results that are chosen based on what you normally search for, not based on that particular search. They are based on what you like on Facebook, what ads you've clicked on and responded to, which e-zine subscriptions you have, and how many online petitions you've signed and for what. The mining of information has become a science and an industry and every time you add a little piece of information to the mix, the design of who you are that lives within the great minds of Dogpile and DuckDuckGo is changed along with it.

The net result – when Ezra Levant and I type the word "atheist" into our respective search engines we are going to get radically different information. When we type in "occupy", the passion we each find is ideologically opposed to the passion the other finds. Our global communications network is deepening the gulf between us to the point that all the information we use to frame our opinions is almost always of the same opinion we had when we headed toward the computer. Our minds are rarely changed by the internet anymore.

## Disintegrated Community Networks

Which brings me to the second negative component at work in society – the disintegration of community networks. While PETA, the animal rights organization, works hard to educate people beyond belief in the proverbial but mythical family-run farm with much-loved animals sharing the shelter of the creaky wooden barn, no single organization has been hard at work helping us understand the implications of our urban planet. It used to be that we lived next door to our neighbor for our whole life. Or, if we moved, it was once, maybe twice. More than that, you were a vagrant. We established relationships, put down roots, raised families, and contributed to the fabric of society by participating in the institutions that held it together – church or synagogue, the Four-H clubs in the country or Rotary and Kinsmen service clubs in the city. Our kids played together, sometimes engaged in and being formed by the global scouting movement. If we weren't growing our own food, we knew the people who were and we called the butcher, the librarian, and the miller by their proper Mr., Mrs., or Miss. When we took a picnic to the park or went swimming in the local creek, we knew the other families there. When wars came and the lists of those killed in action grew longer and longer, we knew every name from the top to the bottom, knew every family affected.

Integration: the coming together of separate items into a cohesive whole. We lived in integrated wholes within our distinct communities. Now, as we struggle toward global "wholeness", the smaller communities in which we live are dis-integrating, separating into components rather than wholes. Our private lives are distinct and separate from our public lives, which may be further distinguished from our professional lives. We move from one place to another, sometimes building relationships around us and sometimes not. Knowing your neighbors, even in densely populated areas, is not a given. One member of my congregation, when displaced by an

154

explosion in her building, noted that the disruption actually helped her meet people she'd been living beside for years and never come to know. For many, our friends are people on television; we become absorbed in their lives in the ways we once became absorbed by the people down the road or across the street. We are swiftly losing the world in which being a neighbor was a natural thing. Perhaps we have already lost it.

## Leadership

There are voices on all sides of every political and social arena pointing to core leadership deficits undermining the efficacy of institutions, organization, coalitions, and governments. Conservative financial pundits point at deficits and cry out for leaders who will slash social programs and save the economy for future generations. Liberals point to the stuffed pockets of the rich and call for leaders who will make the rich contribute to the crumbling social structures that have created and supported the growth of a broad middle class over the past century. Radical leftists cry out for power to be distributed equitably amongst the people, the implementation of which often grinds movements founded in brilliant principles and passions to an ugly halt. Where are our leaders, they all want to know. Where, indeed.

Perhaps, on a global scale, the greatest absence of leadership can be seen in the United Nations. Canadian Justice Rosalie Abella, herself the daughter of Holocaust survivors, has pointed to a faltering of leadership in the arena to which many in the world look for its strength. Abella speaks passionately about the UN's apparent preference for the free flowing of goods over the protection of human rights and cites a growing list of travesties it has overlooked or failed to engage beyond stern editorials and paper-backed comments.

It isn't as though we have been choosing weak leaders. What we've been choosing is a lifestyle that allows us access to everything we've ever wanted at a price we're willing to pay. Petitions challenging Esso and Shell Oil to reduce gas prices so we don't feel the pinch as those prices soar are based in our own lifestyle choices and personal comforts. We want inexpensive t-shirts and running shoes, washers and dryers, iPhones and computers, strawberries and potatoes. These things are acquired through the selling of our leadership to the corporate agenda, not the civic one. Votes, too often bought for a $35 tax break, are so tragically short-sighted they leave us with political leaders who are compelled – by our desires – to give their votes over to those corporations and free trade agreements that can best sell us what we want for pocket change. We are even willing to enslave whole countries to do it, locking populations into low-paying work, and undermining our own independence as we do.

### The Perfect Social Storm

If we were fracturing along left-right lines in our online communications and embedding prejudicial information in our perspectives, these would easily be corrected or at least challenged within a stable, engaged community. Even without that community, strong leaders advocating for moderated change and progress, condemnation of wrongs and distributive justice, could help modulate our responses. But take both of those things out of the equation and you've got 1, 2, 3 Perfect Storm.

Similarly, leverage global communications as they are developing. so we are able to grow because of the diverse perspectives it can expose us to and have those systems morph and develop under a leadership working for the best possible outcome for all of humanity and the loss of community integration might not be so problematic. Outweigh the benefits with the detriments and you've got 1, 2, 3 Perfect Storm.

And, finally in this social storm, we consider a leadership deficit: With communications systems operating in a new and egalitarian fashion and community strong and resilient, the lack of leadership only immediately becomes a catalyst for leadership development along the lines that enhance community. When we don't have those things it is, again, 1, 2, 3, Perfect Storm. Harmful communications harden opinions, communities fracture along lines of intolerance, and the leaders that emerge are financially driven. What a world that would be!

Any one or two of these and we're okay. All three and it is catastrophe.

## Religion

So, here we are at our topic. Religion in the 21st Century. Christianity and how the story evolves. The key word for me is "story". I expect the key word for Bruce will be "evolves." We'll see where those two words lead us.

But before I head off anywhere related to that, I want to draw your attention to things you are intimately aware of, but do it while pulling the thread that connects them so that they all gather together and we can see the overall effect.

### Relevance Depletion

I am proud to be a member of The United Church of Canada. Nowhere else in the world would I be tolerated. That may seem like an incredible thing and I get emails letting me know how incredible it is on a fairly regular basis. But the truth of the matter is that I am proud to be a member and a leader in The United Church of Canada because there are whole segments of the population that are also tolerated in leadership positions within this church. Divorced people, women, gay, lesbian, transgender people. In other denominations, too many of the world's people are seen only as mission fields, as potential candidates for conversion or volunteers with no official title. I am proud to be a member of The United Church of Canada because we ordained women over 75 years ago and the Roman Catholic Church hasn't yet figured out how to do that. I am proud to be a member of The United Church of Canada because we ordained married women in the 1940s, and affirmed a woman's right to an abortion in the 1970s and because we decided to forgive and move on when divorce fractured a clergy marriage. All done decades ago, yet evangelical denominations around the world continue to consider divorce and abortion so sinful that they exclude as unfit for leadership those whose lives have had to face such devastations. I am proud to be a member of The United Church of Canada because, in the 1980s, it embraced the leadership being offered by our LGBTQ sisters and brothers – 25 years later, the Anglican Communion continues to obfuscate on decisions related to sexuality either because it might be against God's will or because it might be objected to by the fastest growing group within its bounds – the African Church. And I am proud of The United Church of Canada now as it struggles with the new definitions of Christianity that you are placing on the table and with which you continue to invite it to engage.

But despite The United Church's continuation as a voice of reason and clarity in the area of environmental issues, empire, community, and relationships, it isn't heard like it once was. People don't pay attention. It is considered irrelevant, its head office staff often miles away in theological discourse from those in ministry on the street so to speak. The Anglican Church follows close behind, speaking almost exclusively on issues everyone can (now) agree about – residential schools, homelessness, the preservation of water, ecumenical dialogue. But each week, fewer and fewer hear and the only time Christianity gets in the newspapers any more is when someone does something so wildly illegal or disgusting that it captures the attention of a broad, opinionated but otherwise uninterested public.

But wait! Aren't the issues of residential schools, homelessness, the preservation of fresh water, the concept of empire and the power of its elite – aren't these pertinent issues nowadays? It's certainly not that they have become irrelevant. In fact, the issues that are discussed at national meetings of mainline denominations are often the very issues that are raised in the alternative press, that get scribbled on poster board during demonstrations, that should turn everybody's head as they are chanted on the way down Main Street, Anywhere. It's not that the issues are irrelevant. They aren't. It's that we are. And so, although we are talking about those very important things, no one is listening anymore.

*Loss of Resource as Community Hub*

I lead in a congregation that grew up in the great suburbanization of a major metropolis – Toronto. During the 50s and 60s, as suburbs were developed, land was set aside for churches and the United Church took full advantage of it. The plan was to put a church across from every school in the neighborhood – free parking every Sunday morning in a lot paved by the Board of Education. It wasn't that crucial that there be parking, though. Everyone walked to church from the blocks around. The significance of having the school across the street was that the church and the school created a double whammy focal point for the neighborhood. And everything was good.

But, as those neighborhoods changed, as new families – often non-Christian families – moved in, and founding families moved further away, the school/church connection grew more tenuous. Church leaders, in the 1970s began to get fewer calls to participate in the leadership of religious programming in the secular school system. In 1989, Ontario led the way in having compulsory prayer removed from the schools in the country. The tie between church and the neighborhood which had up until then been reinforced by the church's relationship with the classroom, was badly frayed.

I don't think we've ever recovered. Added to the distance between church and classroom was the growing multicultural immigrant reality nurtured as an answer to our ever-dropping birth rates. A respect for difference in the religion department whittled back any ideas of proselytizing in the Canadian scene and conversations in congregations were, for the most part, taking place amongst an aging, white, middle-class elite who had never thought of themselves that way but, when they took the time to look around, began to notice. Shifts in denominational approaches took the form of intercultural initiatives and multicultural feasts, all with the

159

intention of keeping the doors open to newcomers, most of whom were no longer white and middle-class and few of whom actually came.

The church that had been intentionally built at the centre of the community was marginalized and essentially discarded by the neighborhoods around it. Oh, the odd family with young children would show up – still shows up – and there are congregations peppered across the country that are, as Diana Butler Bass assures us in *Christianity after Religion*, doing innovative and creative things and holding their own. The Presbyterian Church USA has seen a grass roots program develop called Next Church. Organized by a couple of clergy people who thought they had some good ideas to share, it now draws over 600 people together annually to share best practices, regardless of theology. There's life in them yet, but not the kind of life that will transform the communities around them. That distance remains and grows stronger every day.

Why? Let's look at negative reality number 3.3

### Theological, Liturgical, and Spiritual Masturbation

Don't get me wrong, I love liturgy, ritual, the sound of music lifting harmonies on high. I love the sensual nature of community drawn together to explore, to reflect, to tease truth out of the crevices of our hearts. I love that we can use almost anything on earth to create those moments that rivet us but that again and again, we come back to a few simple basics – water, rocks, sticks, shells, ribbons. Not much you can't do with those five things.

But I lament that what we do in church is too often so tragically one-sided, so oriented toward ourselves. In fact, because it is so insular and so self-serving, I now think of it primarily as "masturbation".

I know, the word is a dramatic one to choose and etymologically, I'm probably on pretty shaky ground. It is likely that the word's roots are related to *mano* for 'hand' and *stuprum* or *stuprare* for 'to defile oneself'. So to defile oneself by hand. So let's skip forward to the more colloquial meaning of the term which, indeed, includes manual stimulation but refers to the pleasuring of oneself. No one else is involved. No need to worry about another's feelings. It's all about you and what you need and want in that particular moment.

And that's what our theology and our liturgy and our spirituality have become – masturbatory acts in which we are all about what we need and want in that particular moment and attend little to what is happening outside.

I first considered the word "masturbation" in relation to prayer a few summers ago. I had joined a group that was exploring contemplative prayer and, while there, engaged casually with another participant. Our experiences of the time in the group were radically different and when I left, although the facilitator had been open to my questions and experience, my prayer partner made it clear that I just didn't "get it" at all – which I'm not ashamed to say, I didn't. But, for her, not getting it meant that I was defective, unworthy, wrong somehow. Her experience during the contemplative prayer programme was so extreme that it left her with the kind of look on her face that was other-worldly. She had managed to get high on prayer. There was a post-orgasmic contentment on her face. You know what it looks like; it's the same look on a baby's face when he's finished nursing. Sated. Sublime, yet deeply, deeply organic.

It had nothing at all to do with the sorts of things I think church is all about – community, building a cadre of leaders who can engage the public on important issues, strengthening interpersonal relationships so that when crises happen, the soul doesn't fall out of the individual or the community. It was too personal, too "spiritual" for it to have any value for the community as a whole.

Similarly, I have participated in liturgical events, highly choreographed rituals that have had the same effect on not just the individuals but the community as well. Bent on feeling something, the leader has led in a manner that has opened the congregation to an emotional experience and then offered that experience to them – usually in some tangible way – which effects a strong and profound change in their demeanour. They become passive, almost unresponsive beyond the acts of the ritual. Sometimes they bow their heads. Often they cry. The purpose of the event seems to be to evoke these feelings, to focus them on the heightened emotional experience until they are brought to a climax of sorts and they, too, have that sated look on their faces.

As congregations lose their grasp on the essential nature of the Word of God, I think they head off in this direction, looking to imbue the acts, the symbols around them with the importance of the God of the bible they no longer revere. Isn't that feeling of union an affirmation that whatever they experienced before, it was greater than the idea of God and not less than it? Doesn't it reinforce that there is a reality of some sort out there that we can connect with, that can affirm us and remind us how important we are? That is what we end up looking for – affirmation and it is absolutely fine, but it isn't what I think church is for.

And theology. Ah, theology. Even this evening there is someone somewhere writing a new understanding of theology that parses the words we used to use and endeavours to make sense of something that isn't real in the sense that you could ever describe it. Theological undertakings are, to my mind, now little more than theo-sturbation – the use of the idea of god to defile ourselves. Holding on to it, rubbing it over and over again to reinforce a concept that is no longer of any tangible use to us seems more than problematic. It seems outrageous.

The upshot of all these public displays of self-pleasuring is that no one wants to play with us anymore. When we are mostly interested in making ourselves feel good, few people are prepared to sit around and watch. If you can interest them in the moves, well, you can play with a partner, but it's still the same, ancient practice transformed for a world so crazy that self-soothing is now the exclusive undertaking of the church.

162

So there we are with the Perfect Storm number 3 – Religion. If it were just a matter of losing our perspective, not being relevant, sitting to the sidelines of the headlines, we could still be part of the very important work of transforming individuals and communities, of pulling people together and into relationships, of creating places where people could gather, explore their depths, and engage in the beauty of life to the fullest extent that the human community is able. If it were just the loss of our capacity to fulfill the role of community hub where people came together to learn, to lean, to engage, we could overcome that with a strong pastoral presence and a program that drew people out of their isolation and into relationships. If it were just the problem with the church itself – its role as a pleaser, as a pleasure-partner, as the source of a personal spiritual high, then the other elements it had chosen to ignore – significant social issues and community engagement would surely be sufficient cause to keep working.

Put all three of these negative challenges together and you have the collapse of what was once, for good or for ill, the cohesive underlying fabric of society and without it, we fragment into family units or isolated individuals, each of us too dreadfully susceptible to the machinations of a greedy corporatist culture, too ignorant of the empire that throbs its life force around us, or the anaesthetization of the matrix, or whatever you want to call it, in which we live.

Hold up your hands, and help me count off the challenges facing us at a result of these three pre-packaged perfect storms.

1) The Earth has just about had it with us. We've kept the taps at full blast and haven't bothered to unplug the sinks. The effluent is overflowing and it's taking its toll. We may be able to enjoy our backyard gardens, but the planet as a whole is cooking and we can't or won't see our role in that process. So it will continue to escalate, ignoring all the supposed warnings and moving on at a pace that has been unimagined.

2) While that happens, we will continue to lose the cohesive nature of our communities. The global challenges, when they finally

come knocking on our doors, will be faced by individuals who have only limited, instinctual knowledge of how to collaborate. In fact, many, if not most of them, will only know how to care for themselves and their families and will turn on those around them who threaten that cohesive unit. We had to climb out of that worldview a hundred thousand years ago in order to survive. Can we do it now? If our leaders are not individuals but dollar signs, do you think there will be any impetus to awaken us to other possibilities or do you think it will be more advantageous for the ruling elite to just keep us fighting one another even if only from within our homes, sitting in front of computer terminals.

3) Unfortunately, the institutions that have nurtured and sustained the narratives that reminded us we could rise out of horror and into cooperation will no longer be trusted to do so. They will long since have lost themselves in the reverie of a masturbatory self-soothing. The communities in which we live will have no common values holding them together and so the value of survival will be the one given most authority. That value uses everything in its sight for its own purpose. If we're going down, in this scenario, we're going down ugly.

In this perfect storm, there is no second chance, no waking up and the nightmare is over, no backyard gardens and pleasure cruises that let us forget the hardship away. In this perfect storm, we go down and what's left when we do is only the legacy of pain we leave to our children.

Almost ten years ago, many of you gathered in a church in Mississauga as we launched the Canadian Centre for Progressive Christianity. It was important work and I spoke about it being time, so obviously time, for that work to be done. We'd been talking about it for decades, or so I thought at the time. Turns out it had been centuries and we in the church had not moved in any significant way that would have tested and built communities of trust and action, trust and forgiveness, trust and keep moving toward something better. We had not moved and so it was time to do so — late, but time. The phrase "It's time" became my mantra and it pulled me forward when, so many times, it would have been easier to do what most of our predecessors had done, stop, set up camp, get comfy, build the house, put down roots.

It's time again but this time not just time to think about church. It's time to think about humanity and what we can do to avert this looming and dangerous storm that is almost upon us. It's time to look to those beyond us and see what they are doing, to put our shoulders, our time, our energy to the work of saving — and I do mean saving — the human family from itself. It's time to pour the energy of prayer and ritual and thinking up complex theologies into doing and creating, learning and making right. It's time to work so hard at getting it right that we risk arrest and detention for doing it. It's time to make real the liberal fairy tale about the "way of Jesus" which so many claim to walk, though too few have really undertaken, a way that puts us at odds with what soothes and sustains us and sends us into a struggle like we have never seen before.

I am not interested in doing church anymore — not church that anaesthetizes while it ignores; not church that takes time away from more serious pursuits; not church that refuses to engage the larger community while it perpetuates a distinctive character, separating it from the everyday stuff of life. I am interested in doing good whatever and however I am confronted with the need for it and whatever it calls from me. I am interested in doing good and offering whatever I can to those around me, around the world, who are also doing good. I am interested only in stilling the storm. Using my heart, my passion, my intellect, my hands, my life. I am interested only in stilling the storm.

is my lens wide enough
to take in the beauty, the desecration
the complexity and simplicity
the regular and the extraordinary ...

is my lens wide enough
to capture diversity, random movement
patterns of exquisite correlation ...
is my lens wide enough
to sense shadow and depth
purpose and passion
dependence and autonomy ...
is my lens wide enough
to see the difference between right and wrong
curved and circular
straight and narrow ...
is my lens wide enough
to see you and me
the distance between us
the ideas that might separate us forever ...[23]

[23] Gretta Vosper, *We All Breathe*, (Toronto: File 14, 2012)

# A Noble Truth

*CCPC Halifax Conference, 2013*

I spoke on Thursday evening about no longer wanting to do church. The institutionalization of our core myth has become, for me, no longer sustainable. I don't believe that the myth that has informed, directed, grounded, persuaded, and soothed us for the last couple of millennia is a story that can take us much further along our evolutionary trail. Indeed, I believe that in the glaring light of science and reason, most of the myths that have sustained the human family are being found wanting and those who have held to them are increasingly disillusioned, frustrated, and angered when they no longer work for them. A study this week showed that less than 12% of Irish students follow religious teachings and 20% identify outright as atheist. Only 45% say they follow a religion because of their parents influence but 40% say they would not share that faith with their children. Bible and book studies meant to engage progressive thinkers in mainline denominations present contemporary, critical Christian scholarship to congregations and groups and often catapult individuals from what is called Stage 3 – Synthetic (Conventional by James Fowler or Pre-Critical Naivete by Marcus Borg) into Stage 4 – Individuative (Reflective or Critical Thinking) before the end of the first chapter. The process, if not done carefully, can be brutal; one's entire worldview is shaken, fragmented, dissolved. The online book study for *With or Without God* has a whole section called Caveats designed to assist the study facilitator help everyone from the facilitator to the minister to the group's participants deal with the reality checks which are going to come hard upon reading that book. Without something to replace one's fractured worldview, angst, disillusionment, fear, depression, and, yes, anger can fill the void. Many are those who fall into Stage 4 and never emerge, spending the rest of their lives angry at the church, their parents, religion itself for lying to them and making them feel like fools. It is not a pretty place, Stage 4. Therefore we seek to rescue and make safe one's emergence into Stage 5 where everything comes back together, this time as myth, and the world is righted again.

But is it? Can we really embrace the truth about our fractured myth – that is, that it is myth – and then live as though it is reality? Can we really articulate a theology that relinquishes a supernatural pre-dawn-of-time god but still sing and embrace all the creative impulse that narrative once gave us? Obviously it can because church leaders around the world have been unleashing creative ways to re-tell the myth, to re-imagine the story, to re-invigorate, re-infuse that mythical deity for the past few decades, fearful that, if they don't, all hell will break loose.

And it might. Without something pulling all the pieces back together, it is true, we get stuck in the disillusionment of individuative–reflective reality (i.e. think for yourself and oh my god, there's nothing there!). It's a frightening place.

Leo Tolstoy, the Russian novelist and philosopher, considered one of the world's greatest writers, fell into despair when, finally, the reality of a nihilistic perspective caught up with him. When chasing after meaning, Tolstoy realized there simply was none.

> *The questions seemed to be foolish, simple, childish questions.*
> *But as soon as I laid my hands on them and tried to resolve*
> *them, I was immediately convinced, first of all, that they were*
> *not childish and foolish questions but the most vital and pro-*

*found questions in life, and secondly, that no matter how much I pondered them there was no way I could resolve them ...*

*If a fairy had come and offered to fulfill my every wish, I would not have known what to wish for. If in moments of intoxication, I should have not desires but the habits of old desires, in moments of sobriety I knew that it was all a delusion, that I really desired nothing. I did not even want to discover the truth anymore because I had to guess what it was. The truth was that life is meaningless...*

*...and there I was a fortunate man, carrying a rope from my room, where I was alone at night as I undressed, so that I would not hang myself from the beam between the closets. And I quit going hunting with a gun, so that I would not be too easily tempted to rid myself of life...*

*...If not today, then tomorrow sickness and death will come to everyone, to me, and nothing will remain except the stench and the worms. My deeds, whatever they may be, will be forgotten sooner or later, and I myself will be no more. Why, then, do anything? How can anyone fail to see this and live? That's what's amazing! It is possible to live only as long as life intoxicates us; once we are sober we cannot help seeing that it is all a delusion, a stupid delusion! Nor is there anything funny or witty about it; it is only cruel and stupid...*

*The former delusion of the happiness of life that had concealed from me the horror of the dragon no longer deceives me. No matter how much I tell myself that I cannot understand the meaning of life, that I should live without thinking about it, I cannot do this because I have done it for too long already.[24]*

---

[24] Leo Tolstoy, *A Confession*, 1882

The present, for Tolstoy, was bleak; the future, bleaker. There was no hope in the perspective that found life meaningless. Beyond belief in the myth that protected him from "the dragon", was only the horror of nihilism. He could not pull that myth back over his eyes. He was captivated by the stark truth that had emerged from behind it and it threatened his every moment.

It is interesting to note, however, that Tolstoy disdained science perhaps because it had destroyed his illusion. As one who believed the great questions could only be answered by discourse within the humanities, his interest in the sciences was to ridicule their inability to answer these questions. "When the ordinary person asks, how should I live, how relate to my family, to my neighbors, and to foreigners, how can I control my passions, what should I believe and not believe, and much else, what does our science answer him? It triumphantly tells him how many miles separate the earth from the sun, how many millions of vibrations per second in the ether constitute light, how many vibrations in the air make sound."

So it is that although he lived and wrote within the same time as did Charles Darwin, he was unconvinced of Darwin's findings, ridiculing them, too, with almost nonsensical passion. From his last letter: "The views you have acquired about Darwinism, evolution and the struggle for existence won't explain to you the meaning of your life and won't give you guidance in your actions, and a life without an explanation of its meaning and importance, and without the unfailing guidance that stems from it is a pitiful existence."

I believe that, had Tolstoy lived to this day, had he been able to explore the sciences that have become available to us, the great explorations beyond Darwin's *Origin of Species* and, in particular, the vast explorations of space, I think his disillusionment with life, his despair, his crumbling at the brink of madness that was his response to nihilism, would have been assuaged, soothed; he would have found hope beyond the horror of his despair. I think we are, many of us, at the same gate Tolstoy arrived at, but we have so much more to answer the despair he encountered there than did he.

The fate of humanity may lie in whether or not we are able to recreate what religion has done for us in the past, find a way to tame the dragon, not pretend it doesn't exist. Here I turn to the work of Loyal Rue, philosopher,writer and professor emeritus at Luther College in Decorah, Iowa.

Rue's work focuses on naturalistic theories of religion. He has studied religions and noted significant truths that lie within them. Truths not about the content of the stories, but about the nature of religion. These truths are that all religions have at their core a narrative. That narrative integrates two kinds of ideas – cosmological ideas – understandings of the nature of reality – and moral ideas – understandings of what matters. The narrative, as Rue notes, con-fuses these two realms, the cosmological and the moral. The result, he names a noble lie. They do not tell the truth about the world, about the nature of reality but the reasons for creating them are noble – they "deceive us, trick us, compel us beyond self-interest, beyond ego, beyond family, nation, race...that...deceive us into the view that our moral discourse must serve the interests not only of ourselves and each other, but those of the earth as well".

The problem facing us now, as faced Tolstoy, is that the noble lies which have entranced us for millennia are no longer doing so. Science should not be able to disprove the myth but more and more, the myths that have entranced us, that have woven together our cosmological and moral universes fracture in the face of a universe that is expanding, of the possibility of life on other planets, of our explorations of reality that are beyond anything the creators of those myths could have known or understood. As the cosmology disintegrates, so, too, does the moral reasoning related to it. Disconnected, the moral universe collapses into a moral relativism that threatens to wreak havoc in human community and our world. So Loyal Rue calls for a new Noble Lie that would present a "universe that is infused with value. And such a universe is

171

ultimately, I think, a great fiction. The universe just is. But a noble lie attributes objective value to it."

I only agree with Rue so far. Yes, we need a narrative that can confuse the cosmological with the moral, but I believe we now know enough that we can create a noble truth, not a noble lie. While it may be true that the universe is indifferent to us, as Rue and so many alongside him have pointed out – Tolstoy included – but it is not true that we are indifferent and it is in that reality that I believe we can fuse the realm of values. It is in that place where our hope and our wonder lie, that we can create a noble truth that can take us forward into hope. It is only in the ravaged remains of the old noble lie that hope is fragile. In the possibility of a new and noble truth, hope is reinforced, made real, made strong.

Let's go there.

> We live, move, have our being,
> on a pale blue dot our eyes have only, in the last few years,
> been able to observe against the expanse
> of an indifferent universe.
> We call it Earth, our home,
> and we are bound to its surface
> by the force of its spinning –
> over a thousand miles an hour,
> it twirls on its axis around a blazing sun.
> A benevolent sun, we can call it;
> it offers its gifts of light, heat, gravitational force freely,
> no expectation in return.

> We exist in a spiral galaxy that,
> when observed in a dark sky setting,
> glows with light.
> Ancient Greeks called it Kiklios Galaxios,
> the milky circle,
> a splotch on the heavens they said was created

when Zeus and Hera,
trying to feed their young son Heracles,
spilled his milk.
It is comprised of some hundred million stars.
A hundred million possibilities
in an area so vast we can only imagine it,
prop the idea up inside our heads
and pin it in place with the art of mathematics.

Our world was birthed 13.2 billion years ago,
again,
the art of mathematics
all that holds the truth of that in our minds.
We struggle with the ideas of four or five generations,
the concept of a thousand years, two thousand, five,
but the idea of 13.2 billion can only ever elude us
with its grandeur,
with its elusive reality existing beyond our comprehension.
And we stand in awe.

Reaching deep, deep, deeper into the universe,
we find the ancients of days, of eons, of seeming forevers,
still birthing stars,
red in the pulsing,
bursting forth of millions of years gone by,
the record of their history reaching our eyes
over light-years of space and time.
Spirals matching that in which we are set,
or Sombreros, millions of light-years across,
flattened by who knows what forces,
ash and chemicals spinning, spinning, spinning,
in what seem to be eternal rings of light.
We are captivated by their beauty,
mesmerized by the images that are now exposed to us.

Once hidden in the depths of night
we see what lies out there,
beyond the realms in which our gods once lived,
beyond the stories that our embryonic intellects
were able to conceive
beyond the questions that still spill from our lips,
unanswered in the deep mystery of what we have yet to learn,
that lie within the storms of what once was,
locked in history unfolding in the face
of all we have left to ask.
Stars that may now long since be dead,
hide within their seed pods,
waiting yet to do what happened ages past.
We are confused by time and space
into believing that what we see is
when what we see once was.


Who are we upon whom the sun rises?
What makes our journey around it something of hope
and not despair?
What draws from us a nobler spirit
than we have shared before?
Anything? Anything at all?
Exploded into being 4 and a half billion years ago,
every element of our earth is composed of the heart of a star.
Hydrogen, helium, nucleosynthesis, and there you have it,
settled into matter, coalescing into pieces –
everything we know, stardust all around.
A mere few thousand years ago –
moments in galactic time, fractions, perhaps of those –
our world spun substance that had not been on this,
our planet home.

Mud, perhaps, the words were never framed...
...there were no thoughts, no ideas,
no names that emerged alongside it
as it turned itself,
spiralling into being along the path of least resistance,
be-coming. Be-ing.
We call it life but then
once started, life bloomed forth –
myriad possibilities all at once,
zillions and zillions of starts and stops,
hiccups and catastrophes,
possibilities and annihilations,
and then, time creeping on,
he was.
Somewhere between 156 and 120 thousand years ago,
in a rift valley, trenched low between the hills,
a single chromosomal variant came into being
and over the course of time, survived.
We call him Chromosomal Adam,
every male on the planet his descendant,
their chromosomes providing a lineage
over the bridge of time.
Perhaps co-existing, more likely not,
the truth does not need such details,
Mitochondrial Eve brought forth life
and it has flowed through eons since.
For a hundred thousand years, she's lived,
her truth borne within us even now.


Their truth is our truth: we are all Africans;
we arose from parentage that links us – blood relatives all.
There is no deeper truth about our reality,
our cosmology than this:
we are all stardust, we are all African, we are all family.

How can this truth speak to us now,
hold us to one another as we have not been held before?
We have been savage over time,
destroying what holds our beauty.
Raging, each and every one of us, against the fear
that we shall one day never be.
We've drawn lines between us,
created myths that fractured our family,
turned us against one another
and brutalized whole centuries of life.
We have divided our home, sealed each other out,
and believed that we could survive thus,
believed that we were safe.
But we were never safe.
Not from ourselves.

New truths call us together, into cooperation.
New truths teach us that when we divide, we destroy.
New truths welcome us into each other's embrace
and we could make harmony there if we would but do it.
But first, there is work that must be done.

Against the backdrop of this cosmological truth,
against our common ancestry,
lie these stories,
tales that have riven our universal soul,
torn us one from the other –
our religions.

Our ancestors pledged their gods to war with one another
and the whole of the human line has paid the price.
Those gods are tired and bloodied.
More bloodied as the days go by.
We, who carry yet the legacy of those tales,

must be the ones who speak the truth of them,
who expose the fabrications that drew them into being,
that spun them of nothing
into something of disastrous proportions
and catastrophic realities.
Against the backdrop of this noble *truth*,
obscuring the possibility of its hope,
is the dark history of religious story
and the caustic hatreds it has bred.
Let us speak truth against these tales,
bring to light the possibility of beauty
against this tarnish of our history
and build a bridge to tomorrow
across which all of us may walk.

Tolstoy was right. There is only indifference in the stars. As they burst us into firestorm, there was no knowledge of doing so. The universe cares not what becomes of us as it carves its reality out in realms we will never touch or know. But we don't live only in the universe or only as part of that universe. We live in realms of our own discovery and creation, for we live in relationship with one another, with ourselves, with our world, with the cosmos. We live in relationship with our planet whether it knows it or not. We live in relationship with the cosmos whether it knows it or not. The indifference of the cosmos on the grandest scale should not impose its indifference upon us or upon our relationships. Certainly, it can be said that what we do to one another makes no difference to the universe or universes, but what we do to one another makes a great and very real difference to ourselves and to the others with and to whom we do it. It makes a very real difference to this, our home. Our moral landscape is not lived out on the planetary expanses that we can see with our telescopes. It is lived out in our hearts and in our lives and so I believe it is not only appropriate, it *is our responsibility* to articulate for ourselves a moral framework that we

177

can con-fuse with the reality of our cosmological framework, a moral truth that we can confuse with our cosmological truth, with the heritage of connection that is ours. A moral truth that, confused with that amazing cosmological truth – how things matter confused with how things are – A NOBLE TRUTH that can take us beyond despair, beyond destruction, beyond the dissolutions of all our former, crumbling structures, to hope once again.

The work of creating our moral framework is already underway. It is being framed by movements that seek dignity for all, that attend to well-being and its creation and preservation against all odds; it is rising strong and vigilant against the corporatist agendas that threaten human rights around the world. It is rising, powerful and passionate in the hearts of those who know what is the right thing to do, not because it is carved in stone or written in an ancient text, but because they can weigh it, feel it, expose it and understand it. Once that is born, they can and will live it, and even find it worth dying for.

*What is our task, then?*

As corporate forces
and those we cannot name
seek to focus our vision on horizons that are too close,
our eyes grow weary.
Unused to distance,
we concern ourselves with what lies close and comfortable.
But this will not do.
Our family, our people, live this whole planet round,
dependent upon its resources,
its future,
its life, if you will.
So we expand our vision,
feel the stretch as our range broadens
and we straighten our backs,
removed from our too small story, our too small cages.

What is our task? What must we do?

Press hard against the forces
that would hold us to the old ways,
that will use them to destroy my sister's hope,
my brother's dream.
Who and what will dampen the hope of my blood,
will limit the quickening if its pulse?
If story, expose its truth.
If institution, make its ways known.
If others, find their hearts,
bring them to the noble truth that is now theirs.
We are all related.
We know what is good for one another,
what leads to well being.
Let us find and share it,
making the world good, healthy, home.
Not because the universe cares; because we do.

## Song for Anyone

You are water, you are stardust,
You are wishes, and you are dreams,
You are feelings, you are thoughts, you are body,
You are always much more than you seem.

And whether I live close beside you,
Whether I ever meet you at all,
I want to live a life that makes yours better,
As you're living out the wonder that is you.

You are comfort, you are distance,
You are presence, and you are role,
You are choices you have made, you are future,
You are broken and yet you are whole.

You are challenge, you are answer,
You are question, and you are strife,
You are chances that you'll take, you are promise,
You are beauty and goodness and light.

And whether I live close beside you,
Whether I ever meet you at all,
I want to live a life that makes yours better,
As you're living out the wonder that is you.
As you live out the marvel,
the wonder that you are.[25]

---

[25] The last stanzas of the reading are from a song written for use at West Hill United Church, *Song to Anyone* © R. Scott Kearns, 2014.

# Empty Tombs, and All That...

Progressions, 2014

Recently, when in conversation with a colleague, I realized that her desire for the familiarity and solidity of meaningful ritual and my self-imposed mandate to only ever offer something original for a particular liturgical occasion, had the potential to leave both of us exhausted and feeling like we'd never quite get it right. Having written and choreographed a powerful and moving service for something – a baptism, the celebration of international Women's Day, the solstice – I still feel the need to write and choreograph something brand new for the next time that occasion comes around. She, on the other hand, feels the need to move away from traditional services and symbols because of her progressive perspective on Christian doctrine and theology, but at the same time desires the liturgical elements of the service to be as familiar and powerful as they always have. Clearly, there are benefits to both and, toward the end of the conversation, we had made our way to that realization.

At those times of the year when people raised in the church are most vulnerable to the traditions of the past, I feel particularly compelled to create something new, rather than be accused of slipping into the clutches of a theology I do not believe. As we approach Easter, I consider the former services I created in my effort to express the underlying energy of the Easter story while tiptoe-ing around its more obvious doctrinal meanings. First, in a classical tone, removing all objects – candles, antependia, plants, banners – and draping the space in dark cloths at the end of the reading of the Passion story and then having all covered with flowers and light on Easter morning. In subsequent years, more artistically, training crêpe paper thorn branches to grow, a foot each week, from one purple banner across to the other throughout the season of Lent, replacing them on Easter morning with banners covered in ribbon lilies the children had made. Later still, more intellectually, shifting the readings of the Tennebrae to the contemporary realities of activists who had surged forward but lost as they attempted to change their own communities and, with them, the world. And finally, more dramatically, a play depicting the creeping awareness that the story was just that – a story – and the implications of that realization in the worlds of those who call themselves Christian. Some were awesome. Others truly sucked. But each new Holy Week propelled the drive forward toward something original, some new creation.

The desire to tell the Easter story in new and creative ways is shared by many who lead whether in traditional or progressive congregations. So is the desire to keep it all the same so everyone knows what to expect, allowing the underlying message to be absorbed fully and deeply. The challenge is to find a way to approach the liturgies of Holy Week so that they can be transformative for both those who yearn for familiar ritual symbol and those who delight in the thrill of ever-new experiences. There is nothing simple about the task in any case, but for the progressive Christian or one who has thought themselves beyond Christian doctrine, it is especially difficult. We need to start by asking ourselves, what is it about that ancient legend that has captivated terabytes of followers over the last two millennia? Are there important elements entombed in it that are still meaningful and important? If so, how can we carry them forward without conjuring Mel Gibson-esque horrifics as we do? I believe when we touch those elements, deeply entombed as they are in the story, how we bring it to our communities becomes less important than doing so with integrity.

In *Amen: What Prayer Can Mean in a World Beyond Belief,* I shared American philosopher Loyal Rue's call for a noble lie that could carry us forward. He looks to the natural world and finds many instances where nature "lies" in order to survive – the moth that looks like tree bark, the cuttlefish that changes its appearance depending upon its backdrop. Rue argues that religion has functioned in a similar way but that as the old myths crumble under the weight of science and critical examination, we need to create a new "noble lie" to replace it. I'm thinking, rather, that it's time for a noble truth and I find that the quest, when applied to our most powerful myths, is almost always satisfying. Noble truths already lie beneath the traditional stories or the wreckage our scrutiny has made of them.

Here is the truth I have found beneath the Easter story. The Passion is a car wreck of a story. For most of us, its details have been worn smooth over time; we are almost oblivious to them. But were we able to rid ourselves of the familiarity that breeds our indifference and read them anew, we would be filled with questions and alarmed by the answers scholars would give us. Crucifixion is appalling and we would be right to be disgusted with the story.

I doubt, however, that it's the car wreck horror of the story that has kept us fascinated. I doubt that it's the promise of salvation, either, though obviously that is a pretty big ticket item, especially if the concept of hell has been graphically engraved on the inside of a believer's eyeballs. What I think makes the passion and resurrection story so compelling is our familiarity with it in our own lives, in the cyclical nature of hope, in the dreams we have watched die, and in those we have boldly picked up from the ashes of another's, or our own, pyre and brought to life once again.

Failure is our truth. We all know it. It comes with the reality of being human. And in the Passion story, we get to watch as one of the most legendary people of all time fails big time. Jesus had

183

garnered followers, raised expectations, travelled the hills and vales of his land fanning the flames of zealots' hearts. He'd approached the seat of the power he was hoping to change (if not see overthrown), and celebrated an anticipated success with an invitation-only party on the eve of his next big move. And then he failed.

There is nothing outrageously unusual about that story. We watched it this past Oscar season, playing itself out over and over again in the images of Victor Hugo's *Les Misérables*. And, when we take stock of our own lives, we recognize it playing itself out there, too. Relationships we thought would last forever, careers we trained so hard to embark upon, ideals we held high in our youth that now lie tarnished, somewhere in the back corners of our minds. We watch, often cynically, as others achieve what we long ago gave up trying to do. We know failure and we watch the story unfold with a deep, intuitive recognition.

Watching another fail can urge the best impulses from us as we offer consolation, encouragement, support or simply sit in a fellowship of grief and lament. Often, there is nothing that can be done to salvage the situation, but the balm of love sown into a broken heart, into a broken hope, is transformative.

Then that other truth is sparked. The truth of a new possibility. The story inspires us to look at those broken dreams and sift through them, searching for those possibilities. Not the possibility of the resurrection of a body; rather the resurrection of a possibility, of a dream, of something hope-filled enough we're willing to work toward it. We'll even sacrifice for it! We create new life out of the brokenness of former dreams.

Long ago and far away – so the story goes – a man had a dream that people could live together and practice compassion for one another. And all about us, to this very day, lie the shards of that dream, sparkling and enticing, sharp and brittle. As you approach this Easter season, may you see your potential in the light of those shards and may you have the courage to pick up a piece and live yourself into the dream that has yet to become reality.

We live in a world of surprise and beauty,
a world of color and complexity,
a world of challenge and delight,
a world of anxiety and alleluias.
We are lifted and fed by the wonder in it,
humbled and laid low by its tragic realities.
In the interwoven moments of its blessing and blight,
we make our lives.

May we, in the spaces between sorrow and delight,
in the moments between harsh reality and beauty,
in the fear that lies in wait between truth and possibility,
learn the art of making light,
that we might shine with peace
and live with hope.
Together on this journey,
we share what comes
with dignity, grace, and love.
May it ever be so.[26]

[26] Gretta Vosper, *We All Breathe* (Toronto: File 14, 2012)

# Impertinent Questions

*Progressions, 2014*

I'm terrible at journaling. Every so often I take the practice up with a renewed vigor, thinking that it is important to write down my thoughts, to record the events of my days, to capture images that I know I'll otherwise forget. But it never lasts. I write for a day or so and then, somehow, never seem to find the time.

It was a failed attempt at journaling, however, that taught me the value of the practice and how helpful it might be if I were able to discipline myself to do it. I was preparing for a move and sorting through the mountains of things that needed to be boxed up, tossed, or given away. In the middle of the muddle, I came across one of my old journals. True to form, it had a single entry in it, a long lament written years before about one of my relatives.

But I could have written it that very morning. Nothing had changed. I had made no progress in the relationship; the intervening years seemed to have offered absolutely no insights. Of course this couldn't have been the case. There must have been interchanges from which I might have learned, opportunities for me to take a deep breath, acknowledge my complicity in the congestion between us, and moved either toward reconciliation, or out of the relationship altogether. Perhaps, had I been diligent about journaling, I would have been able to review the absent installments, convicting myself as I did so, and committing to moving forward in a new way. I might have, but I hadn't.

It can be a humbling endeavour to look back at something you wrote years before. Because most of us would like to believe we are always getting a bit better than we have been, we like to think that over time, our ideas will have shifted. We hope that our everyday experiences have taught us something, that our perspective has stretched both our thinking and our hearts. Going back to something written a decade ago should be a testimony to our growth throughout that time; the many ways in which we're wiser now than we were then.

So it was with eager anticipation that I agreed to review the article I'd written for the inaugural issue of *Progressions*, the journal of the then spanking new Canadian Centre for Progressive Christianity (CCPC). The intent was to explore the ways my perspectives and the issues examined in the article had changed over the past decade. *Progressions* had been launched almost overnight after close to five hundred people attended the CCPC's launch in November of 2004, much to the surprise of its nascent Board of Directors. We quickly took it upon ourselves to respond to the expressed need and published the first *Progressions* issue to coincide with our first conference, *Barriers and Bridges*, held in Oshawa in the spring of 2005 with Jack Good, author of *The Dishonest Church* as our keynote speaker. Those were heady days, filled with excitement and the urgency that need creates.

However, this undertaking wasn't particularly edifying either. As I read my ten-year-old article, "Charting a Course for Change," I found myself resonating just a little too well with what I'd said those many years before. And that's not a good thing. It's a bad thing. To realize so little has changed in the church over that time and only slightly more in my own perspectives is like suddenly looking down and realizing that the whole time you thought you were making progress, your feet have really been glued to the floor; the perception of movement, unfortunately, doesn't get you very far.

Take the opening words of the article, for example ....

*The scholarship informing the progressive movement within Christianity has been around for a very long time. The human construction of the Bible and its metaphoric nature has been well validated. In many instances within mainline denominations, it has also been taught in seminary and theological colleges to those who have long been leading communities of faith. How is it then, that there are so very few congregations that have engaged with this scholarship, or taken it beyond a periodic weekday study group to the Sunday morning worship experience?*

Regrettably, in 2014, it is still too often the case that progressive scholarship is exposed to congregational participants only in weeknight Bible study groups or during pastoral confessions over Saturday morning lattes. What is learned in those critical moments rarely affects the structure, tone, language, and symbol of Sunday morning gatherings. Too many clergy continue to mask their lack of belief in a supernatural deity capable of divine intervention - something many of them learned while at theological college - with traditional language they have carefully redefined for their own personal comfort.

And it is still the case, as noted in the second paragraph, that congregants make it incredibly difficult to create the change clergy want to make.

*When a pastoral leader moves to change anything in the context of a worship service, opposition stands poised at every turn. We have all experienced or heard the horror stories. There are jokes about trying to shift the pulpit three inches to the right, or the ever-vigilant group that confronts the minister when the Union Jack is removed from the worship space.... How much more threatening it is when we attempt substantive change!*

Risking the loss of even one family can risk the loss of the entire endeavour and most clergy quickly realize that their own economic circumstances make it even more challenging to risk halving a congregation. So Sunday morning continues to look, smell, and wag its tail like the old, familiar dog it has always been; and it continues to draw fewer and fewer attendees.

These are trifling concerns, however, when weighed next to some of the other things that have not changed for the better.

> *Religion, by its very nature, is divisive. As it developed, it became a tool for identifying tribes and distinguishing clans. The biblical witness is to the setting-apart of a certain religious group as the route to the Sacred. Both the Hebrew Scriptures and the Gospel have been used to name who is acceptable and who is not, to identify privilege and thus, to establish prejudice. Almost every religion in the world does so.*

As I write, Barak Obama is preparing to speak to his troops about the military action planned by the United Stated against ISIS, the Islamist State in Iraq and Syria. ISIS recently cited American intervention in the affairs of those countries as the reason for the video messages to America and Britain that depict the beheading of a British aid worker and two American journalists. Thus are the deep rifts that religion creates in the human family even more evident today than they were ten years ago. Perhaps that's the result of fear. As more and more of the world edges toward secularism, those invested in religion as a means to stabilize and interpret their realities become more vigilant about protecting them.

In the "Charting" article, I continued, "We cannot afford to live with such tribal prejudice in a world capable of destroying itself." How fervently I wish we had made real progress in that crucial area. I recognize that there are so many things that must be accomplished in order to allow humanity to step away from its divisiveness - global access to education, health care, economic security, and self-determination. But religion is the area we hope to influence and it feels like we have slipped backwards into a world even more deeply divided over religion than we have seen it to be in generations.

And so I believe that the work we undertook a decade ago continues to have relevance, perhaps even more than we believed it did then. Indeed, the conversation we started has rolled through countless living rooms and church halls and will percolate far into the future across this vast land. Starting that conversation is our most brilliant accomplishment and I'm very proud that we were able to both start it and keep it going.

A shift in our focus, however, may be required if we are to pull our weight in the work of transforming the world. Rather than the challenging but much more achievable though elusive goal of creating supportive networks for progressive Christians and providing resources to those wanting to shape theologically barrier-free communities, we should set our sights higher still and work toward the eradication of those human divisions that are based on religion. If we cannot do that without eradicating religion, well, maybe that's something we'll have to consider.

As with my first article in the inaugural issue of *Progressions*, it is likely that the response to this new suggestion will be mixed. Back then, many who read "Charting" were most disconcerted by the questions at the close of the article. Though included to invite discussion in congregations, some readers found them impertinent. I'm certain those readers, and more, will also find the suggestion that we consider eradicating religion deeply offensive.

So I share some new questions with you. These, like those from ten years ago, are intended to provide opportunity for discussions I believe are deeply important to the future of humanity. They need to be asked so we might make choices based on what we know, rather than what we think or what we prefer. I hope, as I did ten years ago, that they will lead to new insights and a revitalized purpose for whatever it is you call church.

190

- If religion is benign, why is it the darling of political agendas that seek to control and oppress groups, communities, or nations? I'm thinking of evangelical Christian rhetoric used to oppress the LGBTQ communities in Nigeria and Uganda, the ravaging of whole nations by militant Islamists, the Jewish covenantal understanding of land that continues to fuel the Palestinian-Israeli conflict, and the casting of the Russian Orthodox Church as Vladimir Putin's new best friend.
- If religion is essential for human community, how is it that anyone is able to live a deeply meaningful life or contribute significantly to the advancement of humanity without any religious beliefs or commitments?
- If the benefits to well-being that are experienced by churchgoers are related to the connections people make to one another and not beliefs, why do so many people think church is about what you believe and not about building community?
- If living compassionate and meaningful lives can happen without religious belief or participation, why is the suggestion that we eradicate religion so offensive?

Perhaps, given ten years has passed, I should be feeling more mellow about the role of the CCPC within the religious landscape and my participation in it than I do. Instead, I'm fired up and eager to find new ways to explore and provoke conversations that will change people's minds about religion, impertinent though they may be seen or experienced to be.

As Sam Harris reminds us in his latest book, "Our minds are all we have. They are all we have ever had. And they are all we can offer others." Let's do it. Let's keep the conversation going, and as we change people's hearts and minds, may we also change the game and change the world.

# Breaking Faith

*Progressions, 2014*

It's not strange that I'm an atheist, a member of the fastest growing demographic group in North America. After all, natural science, anthropology, psychology, sociology, and Biblical criticism, when combined, offer us the insight that, in order to explain reality and quell our fear and helplessness, we long ago constructed an image of a supernatural being, projecting onto it our highest and best (and sometimes worst) characteristics, ideals and activities. Like us but not like us, this god was not merely good but wholly good, not merely powerful, but all-powerful, not merely wise, but all-wise. Like us but not like us, this god could say and do things but also intervene with supernatural power to change things for the better. Once you recognize that reality, it's only a matter of time before you find yourself an atheist.

What's strange about my being an atheist is that I remain in ministry in a mainline liberal denomination after realizing I was.

As an atheist, I do not believe in the god we created, the god called God. Although I did as a child, by the time I reached theological college, I was hungry for another interpretation and was encouraged throughout my theological training to wrestle with, and ultimately, through the study of contemporary critical scholarship, to discard the theistic god, embracing god as a concept rather than as a being. At the same time, like many who have entered mainline denominational seminaries, I was offered metaphorical

192

understandings of religious terms like "god" and stories such as the resurrection. These creative and evocative metaphors helped me make sense of the Christian faith into which I had been born.

At theological college, I'd also owned my responsibility to create and mould metaphor that would present my theological understanding in a manner that suited the context in which I would be challenged to preach it. I was astonished when, after a decade of doing so, I found that most congregants had no idea what my concept of god was, that it was a metaphor for life and the costly love we, at every turn, are challenged to weave into it. All had been wrapped in the traditional language of my faith tradition, steeped in a pre-Copernican verbiage too difficult for them to unpack without the clarity I was inadvertently refusing them.

Furthermore, I began to see that the language I used was fickle, so I began disentangling my understanding of the concept of god from it. Unparsed, it is used as often as a bludgeon as a balm, reinforcing any number of grievous assaults on humanity, the planet, and ourselves. While members and academics within my denomination used god language to demand rights and access for the LGBTQ community, others used the same to argue against the provision of those same rights and access for that very same group. I have seen, as most of my colleagues have, the ugliness that a literal interpretation of scripture can uphold and I can no longer subliminally affirm such theology through the reckless use of terms that reinforce it. Using theistic language metaphorically without disclosing that you are doing so is a form of dishonesty in which I no longer wish to participate, fluent though I once was in its use.

If theological and doctrinal words are metaphors for the vital, human attributes and potentials we initially projected onto the god, God, we must either be perfectly clear that we are speaking metaphorically whenever we use them or we must simply speak without using them. Awe, wonder, integrity, connection, empathy, kindness, justice – these are precious and powerful and necessary all on their own. They need no other authority or validation. If a

193

denomination demands that its leaders must use such metaphorical language instead of direct language to express themselves, then we run the danger of distancing, even alienating the billions of people who cherish these values while participating in acts of justice and compassion for whom the idea of god or the god, God, is profoundly problematic.

I believe, as Don Cupitt says in his latest book, that anyone trained in a mainline theological seminary can be nothing other than a sceptic when it comes to the theistic god called God. That scepticism often takes us far beyond the doctrinally-theistic God who "calls" us to ministry. I suspect that most of my colleagues could not complete the statement, "When I use the word 'god', I mean...." without resorting to anything other than some theistic language. Often the question is avoided by clergy who are uncomfortable walking too close beside a self-professed atheist; because their answers would distance them from the classical theism they want to be seen (especially by parishioners) to believe.

Once you let people know you use the word metaphorically, that you don't mean a supernatural god that can intervene in human affairs or the natural world, things gets challenging. Answering the onslaught of subsequent questions is difficult. I have already heard far too many clergy patronizingly tell me they, too, don't believe in the god I don't believe in while being unwilling to tell me and their parishioners what they mean when they use that word or to responsibly answer their ensuing questions. Neither have they been willing to admit that the reality of the god they don't believe in manifests and supports all kinds of horrors around this world or that it continues to be fed by the liberal assent to believe that the Bible is TAWOGFAT (The Authoritative Word of God For All Time). As the the power of that god abates through liberalism along and the decline of the mainline church, fundamentalist beliefs have often been nurtured by an absence from church ("I don't need to go to church to be a good Christian"). That has bred a frightening biblical and ethical ignorance over generations which will only continue to grow in strength. Such ignorance is something to fear.

I can easily come up with a definition of the word "god" that would allow me to use it as many of my colleagues do, that is, without any compromise of my lack of belief in an interventionist deity. I could resurrect my use of theological language and use it to share my perspectives on the world, personal realities, politics, economics (Jesus against empire, as Dom Crossan would put it), finding myself once more within the comfortable folds of "essential agreement" with the historic doctrines of my denomination. I will not do so because it would be dishonest, allowing others to project onto my words beliefs that I do not intend but that are commonly held.

The congregation I serve makes no claims about what it does not and cannot know. While it does not pledge allegiance to the doctrinal stance of its denomination, it cherishes the same values that denomination has and continues to stand for. Its congregants neither demand nor expect theological language to be used to inspire them in those values. We speak of them directly, not metaphorically. We honor everyone's right to hold the beliefs they choose (there are many within the congregation who are traditional believers nourished and supported in our theologically barrier-free environment). We want to be about the work that moves humanity beyond the beliefs that divide to the unity of purpose that will enable us to live with deep respect for ourselves, for others, for the planet, and for the future.

The board of my church and I reflect from time to time on the possibility that I or we will be rejected by our denomination. Each time we have determined that the cost of creating inspirational community beyond the beliefs that divide is such an important element of our work that we must accept the risks involved. Providing a language that is barrier-free is the only way to do that and, to date, our decisions have kept us focused on that work. It may not be everyone's work and it may not even be recognized by those within our denomination as work that belongs to the church. But I believe, and strongly, that it is work that *does* belong to my denomination and to the wider, liberal mainline church in exactly the same way as was the ordination of women, the acceptance of divorce, the advocacy for a woman's right to choose, the acceptance, celebration and ordination of people of diverse sexualities and gender, the breaking of apartheid, the work of supporting refugees and government policy that makes this nation a safe haven for them, the deliberate call for ecological justice, and work toward a sustainable future, etc., etc.

I hope that my denomination can be a haven for those who are otherwise excluded, exiled, or marginalized by their church because their beliefs are not reflected in doctrinal language or who simply want to come together in community – beyond the beliefs that divide humanity – to struggle toward a sustainable future, right relationship with self, others, and the planet, and to be inspired and supported as they do so. That's the work we are currently about and I will continue to support and nourish that work in whatever way I can because it needs to be done, with or without the god called God, and with or without assent to denominational doctrines. While some may lose sleep over that, others lose sleep when they hear of ministers in mainline denominations tying near-naked 13- year-olds to crosses and dabbing them with red paint. The liberal church is a big tent and those opposed to the work we do within it aren't the only ones who sometimes wonder if that tent is too big.

Whether the stories that framed our faith came from an individual, were woven around much older, Hebraic tales, grew out of ancient Egyptian mythology, were infused with Platonic thought, or were, as was recently argued, crafted by first century Romans, is of little import to me. The bigger question for me is not whether or not I am in essential agreement with the denomination or whether my congregation has a right to remain within the UCC but whether the mainline church itself is able to be honest about the dissonance between the education it provides its clergy and that being received by those in the pews. Can we be honest about believing in a metaphorical understanding of god? Can we survive that conversation with our parishioners and supporters? Can we do what William Sparrow, Dean of Virginia Theological Seminary in the mid-nineteenth century challenged his students to do? "Seek the truth, come whence it may, cost what it will, lead where it might"? That is the question that I have.

I am betting every day that the mainline liberal church has the strength and the courage to be forthright with its members about what we really mean when we use the word "god". I am betting on my belief that it can stop obfuscating and so be able to enter into a meaningful and important conversation about what it will take to save, really save, humanity. And it isn't the god most people think liberal clergy are talking about when they use that word, nuanced and enriched as those clergy believe their interpretations to be. Whether you believe in a divine, interventionist god or not, we (humans, not Christians) are, when it comes right down to it, the only answer we have to the problems that plague humanity today.

I am betting on the mainline liberal church being intentional about being in the midst of the important conversations that frame the human quest, engaging in them with integrity, providing safe, barrier-free space for it to happen, and celebrating those individuals and congregations with the courage to work toward such goals. Whatever it takes to build community around the principle of love being lived out along the edge of a ragged and complex justice and a deeply empathic compassion is what I want the church to work toward. If the fact that I do so without using the word "god" or focusing on ancient stories of a man who may or may not have been an intrinsic part of the original telling of those stories sets me apart from the denomination that taught me to think this way, I am deeply saddened by that but I do not apologize.

If our denomination breaks faith with the crucial and costly work of a compassion-driven justice – work in which it has been engaged throughout the whole of my life – because it chooses

197

instead the reinforcement of exclusive doctrine – it will be I who will have been betrayed, not the church. The church I love and give my life to is not about defending a particular concept of faith but about defending human rights and the planet we live on; not about being doctrinally right but about being compassionate and just and courageous; not about being separate and distinct, but about being engaged and involved; not about requiring uniformity in doctrine but unity in love for one another. I believe our church needs people who think the doctrine it framed so long ago is no longer essential. And I believe such people should be its leaders, calling us toward a future in which we once again address humanity's most pressing issues.

# Charted, Sailed, Celebrated

*Progressions,* March, 2016

A year and a half ago, as CCPC was acknowledging its tenth anniversary as an organization, I reflected on an article, "Charting a Course for Change", that I'd written for the first edition of Progressions. When I think about how that article came to be, it doesn't at all reflect the stately, sedate, forward movement that the word "progression" evokes. Quite the contrary.

Early in 2004, twenty-five people gathered on a snowy afternoon in the lounge at West Hill United in Scarborough. Some of them had driven hours through a dreadful snowstorm to be there. We didn't do much more while we were together than share what had brought each of us into that room. For most, it was a sense of loss related to the evolution of their beliefs beyond the doctrine that had previously grounded them. Through the transition, they had lost family members, friends, the rapport they once had with their minister, and the comfort they'd once felt at church. Everyone there had found their way into the room because their profound experience of isolation had compelled them to reach out to The Center for Progressive Christianity (TCPC), then based in Cambridge, Massachusetts.

The late Jim Adams, founder and then President of TCPC, had a generous spirit and a vision of a global network of organizations that supported progressive Christians. With his encouragement, networks had already been born in Australia,

Britain, and New Zealand. After a conversation with him about West Hill affiliating with TCPC, Jim had invited me to see if there was energy for the creation of a network for progressive Christians in Canada and he was convinced that the best people to ask were the people who had proverbially put their money where their mouths were. So he'd sent me an email list and I'd sent out the invitations. Everyone in the room on that snowy afternoon had sent money to Jim and Jim knew that having done that meant they were people in need.

The stories we shared that first afternoon were riveting and true. We recognized that, woven together, they told a larger story of the need for a network of our own. So we planned another meeting and began the work of creating a charitable religious organization geared to providing a network of support for those who had read or thought themselves outside traditional doctrinal boundaries. We believed no one should be alone in their journey and that whether they were isolated within a large suburban congregation or churchless in a tiny hamlet, they should have a way to connect, and to engage others who shared the realities of their journey. We had our mission and we began the work of responding to it.

That's when things started to speed up.

Before we knew it, we were planning a launch event. Someone happened to know that Bishop John Shelby Spong was going to be in Paris, Ontario, in November. What a fantastic boon it would be to get him to join us as a special guest! Jim helped make the contact and the Bishop and his wife, Christine, helped us set the launch date: November 4th. We filed our incorporation documents, wrote our charitable objects, booked a church hall, and printed up the invitations.

That's when things started to grow.

Initially, we expected a few dozen people but rumours soon added to that number. We began hearing about this group and that who were going to join us at the launch. That someone was driving down from somewhere miles and miles away to hear Bishop Spong.

We started thinking in terms of dozens and dozens and then, finally, in hundreds. Our launch was becoming more successful than we'd ever imagined. The caterers were called. The extra chairs would be set out.

And that's when things started getting a little crazy.

Because, so our thinking went, we needed to think of some way to engage people when they got there. If we were going to have hundreds of people in the room, didn't we want them to do more than just listen to the speeches and go home? Of course we did! So we decided to hold a conference. When? In May! Perfect! And we'd have a great speaker, too. But who? Jack Good! Yes! His book, *The Dishonest Church*, was a very good read and he was available! Terrific!

You do realize, of course, that the root word of terrific is the same as the root word for terror, right? Well, at that point, we hadn't yet realized that. We were poised to emerge as a significant voice in Christianity in Canada but what that meant hadn't crossed our minds. We were too busy paying attention to organizational details and trying to pull off a launch party that people would so enjoy they'd want to opt in for the long haul. Deciding to hold a conference six months after we'd dreamed up the idea just so we had something to put on a card we could hand everyone, in retrospect, seems a reckless idea. But that's only the half of it.

We decided we'd launch a journal at the conference, too. That's the real crazy.

And that's how the first article for Progressions came to be written in the frenzy of a printer's deadline. In fact, a lot of what happened in that first year seemed to whiz by at that same frenetic pace. (More common root words there, I'm sure.) Had I written "Charting a Course for Change" over three carefully-considered weeks or even three more hastily-considered days, I may have been a little less brash. I might not have pressed so hard those impertinent questions to which I referred when I returned to the article a decade later. I might have had a steadier hand and held us to a more sedate passage through those uncharted waters. I might have done things differently.

But the ship sailed into that Sea of Change with its tiller held hard, holding the vessel up close to the wind. The speed was fast; the ride, intense. And here we have arrived, eleven years later, with this, the final edition of Progressions.

There was another piece of writing squeezed into those heady days leading up to the launch. In fact, it was finished on my lap in the car as we drove across the city that November afternoon: It's Time, the speech I gave that evening. I don't use notes when I speak but I was challenged to break with the usual by the formal nature of the event. And so I scrambled into the car with what I thought was a solid draft, but then discarded and wrote and wrote and discarded, reading bits and pieces out loud to Scott as he drove, rewriting because of, or ignoring in spite of, his comments. And then we were there. To that audience of hundreds, I spoke those words and they, like the questions in the Progressions article, remain with me still, despite the hurried nature of the thoughts that coalesced them. And like those questions, their theme, too, has cycled back for my review.

Four times I repeated the phrase "It's time" that evening. In the intervening years since, I've said those words too often to count, sometimes adding the phrase "It's way past time" if the situation was too obviously dire. They have remained in my mind, representative of the whole theme of the event, the movement, the years of work. Emblazoned on my memory, it being time for change in the church was what that speech was about.

But when I return to the printed text of that speech, it isn't the repeated "It's time" that stands out as witness to its central theme. Rather what jumps out, in fact, are the nineteen references to "being called" to a moment in time. Nineteen repetitions of the phrase "we are called" or "being called"; several more in other forms of the same idea. Twenty-four named scholars whom I noted as calling us and countless unnamed theologians, archeologists, biblical scholars, moral philosophers, epistemologists, branded and burned heretics; even those whom the church had simply never acknowledged at all let alone heard. All of these I referenced as calling to us from where and when they lived and what it was they saw.

Clearly, I'd heard the call of those who'd known those uncharted waters about which I wrote some months hence, the Sea of Change that had roiled so long. Those who knew, and some who'd tried it; those who'd drawn plans for the ship, and those who'd fitted her rudder and hoisted her sails. And clearly, too, had I heard the call of those who'd lost their lives battling those seas, and those who yet stood on the shore and sought safe passage. Oh, it was time alright. About that, I had been right. However, it was not simply time to *listen* to those calls; that time was past. It was time to respond. We had reached a moment in time that has long awaited us; a time when we would either respond to those voices or stand condemned for having turned away, yet again. And crazy as it now might seem looking back, that a handful of individuals as unprepared as we so obviously were, would try to respond to those calls, that is exactly what we who launched the CCPC that evening had decided to do.

I believe that the choice we made to begin that work in 2004 was a timely choice. I believe that we pressed ourselves to the work because we knew how important it was. But timely as it was, we also knew we may be too late; too late perhaps to make the difference the church might have made – by years, decades, generations, centuries. We believed we could be the bearers of the stories those many voices called out to us, that we could bring them to the church and ask that it, too, respond. We believed we could encourage the church through the Sea of Change and celebrate the crossing with it.

We must admit, the progress we did make may have been more the result of a configuration of elements for which we can take no credit – access to information, the internet, the increasing plurality of Western societies, the civil protection of human rights and dignities – than anything we did ourselves. Many, many more hands were on the tiller of that ship than the few we laid upon it and we could not have judged the breakneck speed at which it surged forward, conquering vast oceans of thought, challenging practices, addressing ignorance, questioning authority and its privileged interpretations, dismantling dogma as we sailed, and leaving the liberal church drowning in its wake.

It may be that history judges Mark Zuckerberg with more influence over the precipitous decline of religious affiliation than we had. Certainly, deconstructing dogma may have been our intention but destroying the church certainly had not been. A year after the CCPC's launch, however, Facebook came on the scene and within a few short months grew far beyond the simple, social network its founder had imagined. Groups quickly cohered to engage, share, challenge, sell, and deconstruct everything they considered important to them. For the CCPC, that meant that the sheltered conversations we'd provided for on our website became redundant and self-regulating as conversations about religious beliefs and commitment moved onto wider social media platforms and blog sites at a ferocious pace. And while some may have been drawn to belief through their online voyages, it is not hard to imagine that many, quietly accessing provocative truths and the security of anonymous groups, moved in the other direction – away from the belief systems into which they had been born. A generation or two distant from the religious practices of family members, those who even bothered to question religious beliefs had no need to be in a religious community to do so. There would be no surge back to church, even one rinsed clear of dogma and built on a foundation of humanitarian values. Zuckerberg and I may not share a common purpose, but we've laboured hand-in-hand this past decade in our undeclared work of dismantling the need for, and trust in, religious institutions.

The struggle to engage Christianity in such a way as to shift its focus so that it might share its benefits with those beyond belief is virtually over. It's too late. Despite our best efforts to entice them to join us on the journey, that ship never did sail. It remained tethered to moorings we had assumed it would happily, eagerly leave behind: the argument that the Bible was the authoritative word of God for all time, and that doctrine built upon this argument was the creation of human minds, developed for human purposes, and within the quagmire of very human allegiances. For decades, the scholarship that wrested scripture out of the mind and purposes of a god called God and poured forth from the pens of our forbears had been shared within the theological institutions of those very denominations we sought to engage. We had believed them ready to leave those trusted but ill-set moorings behind, but they remained locked in older patterns and were, in the end, overwhelmed by the sea itself.

Rather than wrestle with the implications of that scholarship – all the implications – the liberal church as an institution, refused to slip free. But many of its members heard the same call as had we and they were ready to brave the seas. Whether it was listening to Bishop John Shelby Spong that November evening in 2004, reading an issue of Progressions shared with them by a friend, or absorbing the content of some worldview-dissolving post on Facebook, they heard, they learned, they lamented, and they left. The liberal church is a shadow of its former self, its sails limp and empty, its skeleton crew unable now to even consider navigating the seas of change. In the area surrounding West Hill, the United Church alone has closed four and amalgamated six of its congregations since our work began. Since 2010, twelve of the remaining congregation have hemorrhaged 22.5% of their membership. That is almost a quarter of the UCC's members in a vast and diversely populated area of the city. The remaining custodial congregations are forced into the work of keeping the ship afloat even if it will never sail again, never unfurl its sails to capture a new breeze, or point its bow toward a new horizon.

One of our long-time board members noted at a recent meeting that the purpose of charitable organizations is to address a need in a community or the world. She then noted that while many of them never manage to eradicate the social, health, or environmental issue for which they were formed, those that do, once they have fulfilled their function, have often become so institutionalized that they keep going, shifting themselves away from their original charitable purpose in order to keep the operation going. Then, she said something that silenced most of us. "We've done what we set out to do. This is the only charitable organization with which I've been affiliated that has managed that."

And we have....with a little help from circumstance and serendipity. When I think back to that huddled group of email correspondents who braved the blustery weather and the telling of their pain-filled truths to others they had barely met, I cannot imagine that vulnerable conversation taking place in the same way today. There are too many resources out there for people to be as completely isolated as were these; too many magazine articles, too many documentaries, too many blogs and Facebook groups for that same isolation to exist today. Other networks have arisen – Life After God, and The Clergy Project – for particular journeys beyond faith and belief. The shifting needs of the work may ever remain. But the work of inviting the conversation, creating space wherein it might happen, and resources that could fill that space – we've accomplished that work and done it well.

In the intervening decade, many are those who have worked tirelessly to make information about religion public and accessible, who have bravely taught liberating truths about religion's claimed authorities, and its crumbling proofs. The church may not have wanted to embrace a systemic, role-redefinition – indeed, it may not have survived one – but generations of humanity have been and are ready for the freedom that comes when religious absolutes

206

are set aside. That work is vibrant and ongoing and each of those who have been involved with CCPC will remain engaged in the facet of that work that most excites them.

There is a new work that calls to us now, but not to us as an organization. It is work each of us must do as we feel the need. That is the work of creating the communities that will replace churches as sites where values are named and shared, relationships are built, and well-being is fostered. It should make no difference to us whether or not humanity will survive the disaster of climate change; we can flourish individually and communally as people who love, lean into the areas of need in the world, and find ways of sharing beauty, goodness, and truth with one another. From time to time, we'll fail at that important work, and fail miserably. But if we have built meaningful connections with other people within and beyond our communities, we will survive those failures, learn from them, and move on. The world's needs will not go away by themselves. Our individual needs will not go away. Indeed, our perception of need may do nothing but grow exponentially as we intentionally seek to become aware. It may seem overwhelming. It may even be overwhelming. That must not daunt our conviction that creating beauty, building goodness, and grounding both in the pursuit of truth is a worthy one.

The old paradigm that now splits the world in two – those for whom it no longer works and those for whom it provides a too-easily manipulated contentment – has been humanity's most stable source of security. It claimed a divine being as the source of all goodness and the arbiter of the same. All who believed were soothed by its claims not so much because of the goodness they saw in their lives but because of the goodness it promised – if not in this life, in the one to come.

We can make no such promise and the reality of that weighs heavily on our shoulders. But we can build a world in which we all recognize and take responsibility for being the only source of goodness and the only hands and hearts that can bring it into being.

We can build a world in which we take responsibility for one another's dignity, a world in which the ultimate power is not a supernatural being, controlled and mediated by men who call themselves religious authorities, but is within us. The ultimate power is and only ever has been love. The work of the Canadian Centre for Progressive Christianity may be done but the work of love still needs many hands.

## For Our Humanity

*Tune: Beulah*
*Traditional Hymn:*
*Nearer, My God, to Thee*

Though truth remain concealed, still, it we seek
sure that its benefits outweigh deceit.
Might every mind be freed, all rise with dignity.
For our humanity, still, truth we seek.

Though courage often flags, still, it we seek
sure that our beating hearts must not retreat.
Might we each challenge greet, strong standing with the meek.
For our humanity, courage we seek.

Though peace seems far away, still it we seek
sure that our warring cries, we must defeat.
Might we sing songs of peace, a brilliant future see.
For our humanity, still, peace we seek.

Though justice fall behind, still, it we seek
sure that its lengthy arc, bends t'ward the weak.
Might we make real the dream: one just society.
For our humanity, justice we seek.

© 2015 gretta vosper

## Acknowledgements

I never imagined that I would be able to get this book together to share with you. So much has happened over the past thirteen years, much of it recorded in these speeches and articles. I so wanted to share them with you so that you could walk the path once again, if you've walked it already. Or, for those of you for whom this work is new, to journey alongside those who traveled an unknown road demanded by this work.

I am incredibly grateful to Christopher Payne without whom this book would not have happened. Seriously. I would not have even thought of putting this book together or had the faintest idea how to do it, if it had not been for his bold and big challenges and the incredible support with which he backs those challenges up. He has been an inspiration and this book would not be in your hands without his encouragement and guidance. He has been an wonderful gift to me over the past months.

But for the content, there are many more to whom I must express gratitude. Taking on the creation of a new organization with the purpose of creating connections between people isolated by one of the largest institutions on the planet – Christianity – is daunting. But those who gathered in 2004 to do just that and who worked diligently across the next dozen years accepted that challenge. In so doing, they brought people together, opened up conversations, launched book study groups, labored over article copy procured from people who too often failed to meet deadlines (hmmmm.....) and ensured that those who had educated themselves beyond belief – often with the help of the church – were acknowledged, affirmed and engaged. It was a brave thing to do and I am grateful to all who helped make this important work happen.

For reasons all will understand, I'm not naming names. Despite my expectations that the liberal church would open itself to those its regular language excludes, the opposite has happened in my denomination. So those who were happy to participate quite publicly early on, with the direction my own denomination has taken, may not have the same willingness to be easily identified. To respect their anonymity, then, I have chosen to acknowledge without sharing names unless I have express permission to do so. You know who you are and you know that you have appreciation from the bottom of my heart. Perhaps, one fair day, you can open this book and be proud to see your name written here.

To begin with, literally, I thank those who sat around the lounge at West Hill United on that snowy winter day in January 2004. Just showing up was an act of courage. Your commitment and engagement created the passion that turned into the Canadian Centre for Progressive Christianity. Those who worked to incorporate the new organization and then help it achieve charitable status – no mean feat; you provided skills and oversight that allowed the rest of us the confidence to keep going. Those who took positions as Directors on the corporation's Board and managed it over the years through times of growth and times of challenge, your presence and work allowed us to continue. With the creation of a forum website, a challenge several years ago, some of you regularly monitored and engaged with participants. Your work was so important for us. Some of you held fast through the entire history of the organization. I am amazed at the effort you put in and the dedication you showed. I cannot express my appreciation for your constancy. It humbled me and all of us.

And my travel friend. You made every CCPC trip fun while still making sure that I was in the right place at the right time with the right speech ready to be delivered. Those were some of the most organized days of my life! Thank you so much!

I am so so so grateful to West Hill United Church which sheltered the early days of the organization (before it was even named), providing several of its key organizers, offering space, and being the crucible for the work of creating a theologically barrier-free congregation. So much of what I have offered over the years was first tested by you, the people of this amazing congregation. Your participation has cost you much over the years and yet you consistently speak to me of the benefits, the richness we know there, and the passion you have for the work. Thank you for your vast understanding, permission, willingness, and courage. You are awesome.

My mentor, Bishop John Shelby Spong, changed my life beginning with the first day we met at the launch of the CCPC. Along with his wife Christine, he has encouraged me, calmed me down, introduced me to my publisher, and reminded me to speak when it might have been easier to stand down. I value their presence in my life more than I can ever express.

Finally, my appreciation for Scott's constant presence throughout these years cannot be expressed. Often left to hold the fort at West Hill while I shared the CCPC's work elsewhere. He used the years to create some of the most beautiful music being created in church these days, no exaggeration. You will see his lyrics in a couple of places in the book. That he is my partner often washes over me and leaves me in awe. I know we could never have done what we have done without his support, his brilliant mind, and his extraordinary musical gifts. I couldn't be more loved and that truth has been my most constant strength.